Walter W. (Walter William) Skeat

Pierce the Ploughmans crede (about 1394 A.D.)

Walter W. (Walter William) Skeat

Pierce the Ploughmans crede (about 1394 A.D.)

ISBN/EAN: 9783742862600

Manufactured in Europe, USA, Canada, Australia, Japa

Cover: Foto ©Paul-Georg Meister /pixelio.de

Manufactured and distributed by brebook publishing software (www.brebook.com)

Walter W. (Walter William) Skeat

Pierce the Ploughmans crede (about 1394 A.D.)

Pierce the Ploughmans Crede,

to which is appended

God spede the Plough.

BERLIN: ASHER & CO., 13, UNTER DEN LINDEN.
NEW YORK: C. SCRIBNER & CO.; LEYPOLDT & HOLT.
PHILADELPHIA: J. B. LIPPINCOTT & CO.

Pierce the Ploughmans Crede

(ABOUT 1394 A.D.)

TRANSCRIBED AND EDITED FROM MS. TRIN. COLL., CAM., R. 3, 15, COLLATED WITH MS. BIBL. REG. 18. B. XVII. IN THE BRITISH MUSEUM, AND WITH THE OLD PRINTED TEXT OF 1553;

TO WHICH IS APPENDED

God spede the Plough

(ABOUT 1500 A.D.)

FROM MS. LANSDOWNE 762;

BY THE

REV. WALTER W. SKEAT, M.A.,

LATE FELLOW OF CHRIST'S COLLEGE, CAMBRIDGE AND EDITOR OF "LANGLAND'S VISION OF PIERS PLOWMAN," "LANCELOT OF THE LAIK," AND "THE ROMANS OF PARTENAY."

LONDON:
PUBLISHED FOR THE EARLY ENGLISH TEXT SOCIETY,
BY KEGAN PAUL, TRENCH, TRÜBNER & CO.,
PATERNOSTER HOUSE, CHARING-CROSS ROAD.
1867.

[Reprinted, 1895.]

Richard Clay & Sons, Limited, London & Bungay.

CONTENTS.

PREFACE. § 1. The present a *new* edition. § 2. Description of the editions. I. By Wolfe (1553); II. By Owen Rogers (1561); III. By Dr Whitaker (1814); IV. By Mr Wright (1832); reprinted in 1856. § 3. Investigation of the MS. in the Brit. Museum. § 4. The Trinity MS. § 5. Results. § 6. Restoration of the original text. § 7. Printed in long lines. § 8. Some account of the poem. § 9. Books for consultation. § 10. The rise of the Mendicant Orders. § 11. Date of the poem. § 12. The author. § 13. The "Complaint of the Ploughman," or "Plowman's Tale." § 14. Dates of both poems. § 15. Fine passages in the poem. § 16. The five new lines now first printed. § 17. Glossary to the edition of 1553 .... i—xix

PIERCE THE PLOUGHMANS CREDE 1
Notes to the "Crede" 33
Glossarial Index 56
Index of Names 68

GOD SPEDE THE PLOUGH 69
Notes to "God spede the plough" 73
Glossarial Index 75

PREFACE.

DESCRIPTION OF FORMER EDITIONS, AND OF THE MSS.

§ 1. THE present edition of "Pierce the Ploughmans Crede" may fairly be said to be almost entirely a *new* one; the *Text* being new throughout, as is also a large part both of the Notes and Glossary. In order to explain whence this new text is derived, it will be proper to give, first of all, an account of former editions.

§ 2. I. The *first* edition, and the most important, is that of 1553. The title-page contains solely the words "Pierce the Ploughmans Crede" within a square space in the midst of a wood-cut illustrating the story of Pyramus and Thisbe; the picture being by no means unsuitable for Chaucer's version of the poem. The wood-cut is clearly of continental workmanship, and a copy of the lower part of it, not very well executed, may be seen at p. 96 of "A book of Roxburghe Ballads," edited by J. P. Collier; 1847. The colophon, on a separate leaf, is—IMPRINTED AT LONDON BY REYNOLD WOLFE, ANNO DOMINI M.D.LIII. It was no doubt issued owing to the success of "The Vision of Piers Ploughman," which had been printed by Robert Crowley, in 1550; and considering the tone of the poem, we may safely conclude that it was issued in the early part of the year 1553, while Edward VI. was still alive; for he died on the 6th of July in that year. The reign of Mary was not favourable to its existence, and copies are now very scarce.[1] I have made use of a copy preserved in the Cambridge University Library, and readings

[1] See account of the *third* edition.

from this are denoted in the foot-notes by the letter C. It consists of only 16 leaves, 4to.

II. Elizabeth having succeeded Mary, the poem was again in request. The title-page of the *second* edition has on it merely the words "Pierce the Ploughmans Crede," and no more, the wood-cut having disappeared. It was printed at the same time as "The vision of Pierce Plowman," and often bound up with it; and we learn from the title-page of the longer poem that it was "Imprynted at London, by Owen Rogers, dwellyng neare vnto great Saint Bartelmewes Gate, at the sygne of the spred Egle. ¶ The yere of our Lorde God, a thousand, fyue hundred, threscore and one. The .xxi. daye of the Moneth of Februarye."[1] This edition of 1561 is simply a reprint of that of 1553, and clearly not copied from the MS. It preserves the misprints of the first edition, and adds more to the number; and is therefore considerably inferior to it.

III. In 1814, Dr Whitaker reprinted the first edition of 1553. His object was clearly to produce an *exact* copy of it, and he accordingly used black-letter type and such various marks of contraction as appeared in the old book. It may be considered as a great success, as it accurately reproduces every peculiarity, every misprint, and every stop and mark; so that any one who wishes to have a good copy of the first edition may safely buy this instead, at a far lower price.[2] I have carefully collated these two, and here give the few corrections which any one who buys Whitaker's edition should make.

In the address "to the Reader," last line, the *J* should be an *I*.

Fol. C ij, l. 5 from bottom, the words "more money" are, in the oldest edition, run together into one.

Fol. D iij, l. 15; for "swich" read "swhich."

Fol. D iij, *back*, l. 7; for "swich" read "swhich."

Id. l. 21; for "And" read "Any."

---

[1] The "Crede" has also a colophon, agreeing with this, but which does not give the date.

[2] The title-page bears—"Pierce the Ploughman's Crede. London. Reprinted by T. Bensley, Bolt Court, Fleet Street, for Lackington, Allen and Co., Finsbury Square; and Robert Triphook, St James's Street. 1814."

Fol. D iiij, l. 10; for "laiche" read "latche;" though the *t* in the old edition is very indistinct.

Fol. E j, l. 13; for "feid" read "feid."

Fol. E ij, *back*, l. 3 from bottom; for "Abbots" read "Abbottes."

Fol. E iij, l. 13, read "hōly;" in Whitaker's edition the stroke is shifted, and appears above the *l*.

These corrections made, the sole points of difference are, (1.) that the folios do not correspond; (2.) that the words printed in the *margin* of the old edition are printed by Dr Whitaker in large red letters, to receive which he has made breaks in the continuous text; and (3.) that Dr Whitaker employs *red* letters for the proper names. I should add, that all three editions have a short glossary at the end, made apparently by Reynold Wolfe, for which see p. xix.

IV. Mr Wright, in 1842, reprinted the "Crede" at the end of his excellent and handy edition of the "Vision," the publisher being William Pickering; of which a second and revised edition appeared in 1856, published by J. R. Smith, at a very moderate price. Mr Wright corrected most of the more obvious mistakes, so that his edition is very good and useful, and has been of very great service to me, and I here express the obligations to him which I thus lie under. It is therefore with no wish to detract from it, but only for the reader's information, that I here state that I have observed several misprints in it which are mere printer's errors, but where the edition of 1553 is quite correct. Thus at p. 456, l. 182, "Slaughte *in* her ende" should be "Slaughte *is* her ende;" ten lines lower, "Put" should be "But;" and fourteen lines lower still, "Minorities" should be "Minorites." I am of course speaking of his revised edition, and I am induced to believe that the revision of the "Crede" may have been somewhat hurried, as I have observed no such traces of haste in the "Vision."

§ 3. Besides the help thus afforded, we are much indebted to Mr Wright for the following sentence in his Introduction. He says, "I know only of two MSS. of the Creed of Piers Ploughman, one in the British Museum (MS. Reg. 18 B. xvii.), the other in the Library of Trinity College, Cambridge, both on paper, and written long after the date of the printed editions, from which they appear to have been copied." But for this notice, I might have overlooked the Trinity MS., as only the British Museum one is mentioned in Warton. After reading the above, I thought I could not do better than investigate these MSS. closely ; they might perhaps give *some* assistance. The result was surprising, certainly. First of all, it should be noted that Warton speaks of the British Museum MS. as "*not much older than the printed copy,*" and this is certainly the more correct opinion ; the British Museum authorities whom Mr Furnivall consulted, declared it to belong certainly to the reign of Henry VIII.; and that it was *not* copied from the printed edition became more and more obvious the more I read of it ; it soon appeared to be *much more correct*,[1] and I was myself quite satisfied that it was an independent and valuable text. At the same time, it occurred to me that a very obvious proof of its independence would appear in its containing anywhere additional lines ; and, after hoping to find some for a long time in vain, at last *five new lines* appeared, very near the end. These extra lines are of such importance that I have fully discussed them farther on.[2]

§ 4. But an examination of the Trinity MS. surprised me more still. The handwriting is late enough, certainly ; possibly after A.D. 1600. But a curious circumstance at once arrests attention, and that is, the continual use of the Saxon letters ȝ and þ, where the B. M. MS. and the printed editions have *gh* and *th*. It is clear that no man copying from a printed book would systematically make these alterations from one end of the poem to the other, and it is not very likely, even if he did, that he would never make a mistake over it. It is, in fact, obvious, that the Trinity MS. was copied from a much older MS. which is now lost, and this appears farther from noticing the nature of the few blunders that occur in it. Thus, in the first page, the copyist, not quite seeing the difference between a *y* and a þ, miswrites one for the other ; but he soon *gets over this*, and *afterwards does it right*. Again, seeing the word "wiffen" before him, he copied it "willen," a mistake easily made in copying from

---

[1] I mean, as regards *readings*. But the scribe of this MS. took no pains to preserve the true *spelling ;* he has altered it throughout at pleasure, always for the worse. Many erasures and alterations occur in it, also always for the worse.

[2] See p. xvii.

manuscript. Very many more proofs might be adduced, but it will probably be quite sufficient to add, further, that the *five extra lines* spoken of above *appear in this MS. also.*

§ 5. The results of the investigation, which seem to me beyond all controversy, are these:

(1.) The British Museum MS. is older than the printed copy, and not copied from it.

(2.) The Trinity MS. is later than the printed copy, but is not copied from it.

(3.) Both MSS., and also the early printed text, are *all* copied from *one and the same* MS., a very good one, possibly even of the very last years of the fourteenth century, and which is now either lost or not forthcoming. The extreme similarity of these three texts cannot be otherwise accounted for.[1]

Besides which, it is farther evident that the Trinity MS. is the best copy of the three,[2] and I have therefore used it for the text throughout, copying it literally and exactly, marking the expansions of contractions by italics. The only alterations made in it are, the use of capital letters to denote proper names where the MS. has often small letters, and some corrections which have been furnished by collation, which are all noticed in the foot-notes, and which, in every case where the correction is at all important, are pointed out by the use of square brackets. In the foot-notes, this MS. is denoted by the letter A.

The British Museum MS. is the second best copy, and is denoted

---

[1] I think I may be allowed to judge of this, from having examined, more or less, some thirty MSS. of the "Vision of Piers Ploughman." Even when such MSS. agree very closely indeed in *all other* respects, they scarcely ever contain the *same number of lines*. It is a peculiar defect of MSS. in alliterative verse that lines are frequently omitted. Yet these two MSS. and the early printed text run line for line and word for word throughout; except in the one instance of the five extra lines, which can be well accounted for.

[2] The best copy, in the present case, is to be judged of, not by the date, but by traces of the care taken by the copyist. It is clear that the writer of the Trinity copy was a scrupulous and painstaking antiquary, who carefully put down what he saw before him. It is written on some extra leaves at the end of a copy of Chaucer. The Chaucer had some leaves lost at the beginning, but the missing portion has been carefully supplied *by the same hand* that copied the "Crede." The press-mark of the volume is R. 3. 15.

by the letter B in the foot-notes, the letter C (as already stated) meaning the edition of 1553. Attention is drawn to those readings of C which are *most corrupt* by marking them, in the foot-notes, with an asterisk. *The number of these is about* FORTY.

§ 6. By collation of these three, we are placed in almost as good a position as if we had the original old MS. before our eyes. I have little doubt but that the reader will be well-pleased to find that he is in possession of a sound and trustworthy text, much superior to that of 1553, because it is free from the modifications of spelling which the old printer often made, and because the misprints of that edition have been quite eliminated, and the true sense restored in several formerly doubtful passages. Indeed, the only points now open to doubt are very few; I somewhat mistrust the word *euelles* at l. 242; the word *wlon* at l. 736; and I suspect that, as is usual in alliterative poems, some lines were omitted even in the original; for the transition from ll. 69, 648 to the lines following them is rather too abrupt. I subjoin specimens of Texts B and C.

B. SPECIMEN OF THE BRITISH MUSEUM MS. (BIBL. REG. 18 B. XVII.)

Crose and curtys crist thys begynnyng spede,
For the Fathers Frendshype that Formyd hevin,
And throughe the speciall sprite that sprang of hem twayne,
And all in one godhed endles dwellyth.
A, and all myn A. b. c. after haue I lernyd,
And partes in my pater noster ich poynt after other,
And after all, myne Ave mare, Almost to the ende, &c.

C. SPECIMEN OF THE OLD EDITION OF 1553.

Cros & curteis Christ this begynnyng spede,
For the faders frendshipe, y^t fourmed heauen,
& through ye special spirit y^t sprōg of hē tweyne
And al in one godhed endles dwelleth :
A, and all myn A, b, c, after haue I lerned,
And patres ī my pater noster, iche poynt after other,
And after al, myne Aue marie, almost to the end, &c.

§ 7. I have printed the text in long lines, because all the copies are so written and printed, except only Mr Wright's edition. Mr Wright argues for the printing in short lines, in his Introduction, p. xxxii., because of the construction of the Anglo-Saxon verse, &c., and says that "a modern editor is wrong in printing the verses of Piers Plowman *in long lines, as they stand in the manuscripts*, unless he profess to give them as a fac-simile of the manuscripts themselves, or he plead the same excuse of convenience from the shape of his book." The italics are my own; and I will here only say that I do profess to give a fac-simile of the MS., and that I do plead also the excuse of convenience. He also observes that, "in either case, he must carefully preserve the dots of separation in the middle of the lines, which are more inconvenient than the length of the lines, because they interfere with the punctuation of the modern editor." This then I have done, though I have not found it inconvenient. On the contrary, I think it a great convenience. The dot denotes a pause in the rhythm, which very often indeed is coincident with a pause in the sense or with a comma, and thus indicates a certain indefiniteness in the pause, for which it is convenient to have a mark; and it is such a one as we are all accustomed to in the colon used in the Prayer-Book version of the Psalms. A semi-colon in the middle of a line is very rare; if it be required to denote one, we have only to print ; · and it is done. I was induced to use the inverted full stop for this purpose, because it is very easy to print in any sized type, and because the use of a colon produced too heavy an effect, and did not look well. It is right to add that, in the edition of 1553, which is very badly punctuated,[1] the central rhythmical pause is denoted by a comma in about five lines out of six. In MS. B it is neglected; but in MS. A it is, for the most part, *carefully preserved*, and denoted by a kind of colon. Here, then, the superiority of this MS. is once more indicated.

§ 8. SOME ACCOUNT OF THE POEM.

The reader may consult with advantage Warton's History of English Poetry (vol. 2, p. 123, ed. 1824), upon this subject. In a copy of the "Crede" in Warton's possession, was a short abstract of

[1] Two or three passages, unmeaning in all former editions, have been made clear in the present one by a slight change in the punctuation.

the poem in the handwriting of Alexander Pope, to whom the book once belonged. As anything written by Pope has an interest of its own, I here quote it.

"An ignorant plain man having learned his Paternoster and Avemary, wants to learn his creed. He asks several religious men of the several orders to teach it him. First of a friar Minor, who bids him beware of the Carmelites, and assures him that they can teach him nothing, describing their faults, &c. But that the friars Minors shall save him, whether he learns his creed or not. He goes next to the friars Preachers, whose magnificent monastery he describes: there he meets a fat friar, who declaims against the Augustines. He is shocked at his pride, and goes to the Augustines. They rail at the Minorites. He goes to the Carmes [Carmelites]; they abuse the Dominicans, but promise him salvation, without the creed, for money. He leaves them with indignation, and finds an honest poor PLOWMAN in the field, and tells him how he was disappointed by the four orders. The ploughman answers with a long invective against them."

To this Warton subjoins an account of the mendicant orders, occupying about eight pages, which should be consulted.

§ 9. Good accounts of the rise and spread of the mendicant orders are abundant. The reader may, for a general view of them, consult with advantage Massingberd's History of the English Reformation, chap. vii.; Southey's Book of the Church, chap. xi.; the very interesting preface to the "Monumenta Franciscana," by the editor, Professor Brewer; the excellent life of S. Francis of Assisi, in Sir James Stephen's "Lectures on Ecclesiastical Biography;" Mrs Jameson's "Legends of the Monastic Orders;" and almost any Church History. I shall here only touch on such points as have *special* reference to the poem.

§ 10. The degeneracy of the monks began to draw attention at an early period; and, in particular, St Hildegardis, abbess of St Rupert's mount, near Bingen,[1] addressed to them words of solemn warning, in the shape of prophecies which announced that still greater corruptions were to come, and would be punished by shameful disgrace and ruin. Very nearly at the same time, viz. during the reign

---

[1] See l. 703, and the note to it.

of Henry II., appeared the masterly Latin satires of Walter Map, who was particularly severe upon the Cistercian Benedictines, of whom he saw rather too much.[1] Two of his poems, "The Apocalypse of Bishop Golias," and "The Confession of Golias," contain most keen and brilliant satire. They are distinguished by a peculiar subtlety, which has not always been understood. Thus, when Map introduces a drunken priest revealing the depth of his degradation by uttering the oft-quoted stanza,

"Meum est propositum in taberna mori :
Vinum sit appositum morientis ori,
Ut dicant cum venerint angelorum chori,
'Deus sit propitius huic potatori'"—

this has seemed to many a mere jovial toper's song, and nothing more. But such was not the view taken, we may fairly conclude, by the author of the "Crede." He can perceive only two possible causes of the rise of the mendicant orders; either the simple supposition that Satan founded them, or else that they originated, in no slight degree, from the popularity of the "Golias" poems.[2] He suggests that the subtlety of Map's satire was such that the monastic orders were brought into utter disrepute, and therefore the mendicant orders arose to supersede them. That the influence of the "Golias" poems was so great as this may well be doubted, especially when we remember that the new orders commenced on the continent, not in England. At the same time, it is equally certain that our author is not far wrong; it is quite clear that the rise of the mendicants was due to an attempt made (and which was at the first outset a successful one) to infuse a new spirit of piety and humility into the church, and to regenerate it by efforts of great self-denial and devotion. The character of St Francis seems to me to be in many respects beyond all praise; an enthusiast he was certainly, but noble, self-sacrificing, and pure in heart and aim in the highest degree. To give but one instance : we read that he had the greatest natural repugnance to the sight of a leper, yet he forced himself to eat out of the same dish

[1] See Professor Morley's English Writers; vol. i. p. 584.
[2] See l. 179, and the note to it.

with one whom no one could see without loathing, and afterwards devoted himself especially to an attendance upon the leper hospitals, enjoining his followers to do the same. Such an act was a noble example of mercy and humanity; and, had his followers really followed his rules, they might have done well for a long time.[1] But St Francis was clear-sighted enough to see how liable all human institutions are to perversion and decay, and this reflection kept him in continual sadness. "Cheerless and unalluring is the image of Francis of Assisi: his figure gaunt and wasted, his countenance furrowed with care, his soul hurried from one excitement to another, incapable of study, incapable of repose, forming attachments but to learn their fragility, conquering difficulties but to prove the vanity of conquest, living but to consolidate his order of Minor Brethren, and yet haunted by continual forebodings of their rapid degeneracy."[2] And this too surely came to pass; and however bad may have been the state of the monks who forgot their vows of renunciation of the world, it was not long before the state of the friars became far worse. Their greed, their selfishness, their love of magnificent buildings and, very often, of delicate clothing which they concealed under their rough cloaks, their insolence, their pride, their self-righteousness, made them fair objects of satire, which was levelled against them most unsparingly by many, and especially by Wycliffe and his followers. This is nowhere shewn more clearly than in the story quoted by Southey,[3] shewing how the friars waited on Wycliffe once at Oxford when he was supposed to be sick unto death, when he "raised himself on his pillow, and looking at them sternly, replied, I shall not die, but live still further to declare the evil deeds of the friars!" And thoroughly did he fulfil his own prediction.[4] They retaliated on him and his followers, as might be expected; and were particularly active in trying to secure the condemnation of Walter Brute,[5] when he was examined by the Bishop of Hereford, on a charge of heresy.

§ 11. The mention of the last circumstance helps us to fix the

---

[1] See ll. 511, 514.   [2] Sir J. Stephen: Ecclesiastical Biography; p. 95, 4th ed.
[3] Southey: Book of the Church, p. 193; ed. 1848.   [4] See ll. 528—530.
[5] See l. 657.

date of the poem; it is spoken of in the past tense,

"Byhold opon Wat Brut · whou bisiliche þei *pursueden*,"

and the writer seems to hint that they did not very greatly succeed, and were obliged to content themselves with preaching against him, and calling him a heretic. Walter Brute was examined more than once, and he was on his trial from time to time, from A.D. 1391 to 1393. On Monday, October 6, of the latter year, he submitted himself to the bishop of Hereford, contriving rather to allow that his opinions might be overruled by the church than offering to recant them explicitly, so that he was less severely treated than his opponents had hoped and expected. At the same time, this circumstance, though past, was no doubt still very fresh in the minds of all, for the present tense is used in ll. 659, 660; and we also gather that, though the friars wished to see heretics burnt, there had been no instance as yet of any such event. Hence the poem was certainly written after the latter part of 1393, and before 1401. But we may come much closer than this to the date; for the allusion to flattering *kings* in ll. 364, 365 no doubt refers to Richard II., who was still alive. Indeed, had the poem been written in the year of his death, or just after it, we might fairly expect to find some allusion to it, so that our lower date now becomes February, 1400. Hence internal evidence alone suggests some year in the series 1394—1399 as the year of composition.

§ 12. But this inquiry is closely connected with another, viz., what is known of the author? We know certainly that he was an avowed Wycliffite, that he was *not* the author of the "Vision of Piers Plowman" (which was partly written in A.D. 1362),[1] but that he imitated the metre of that poem, and, to some extent, the satirical tone of it. Besides this, he clearly took the plan of his poem from the "Vision;" the way in which he wanders about seeking some one

---

[1] The vocabulary of these two writers is very different, and their peculiarities of style and phrase are quite unlike, whilst at the same time they are very characteristic. Nor are their views alike on all points. There is nothing to shew that Langland was a follower of Wycliffe, though he may have regarded his teaching with complacency. But we need not infer that Langland was now dead, or that he wrote no more than the "Vision." A poem on the "Deposition of Richard II." reproduces *all* his peculiarities, and betrays, as I think, the hand of the master.

to teach him his Creed is copied from the description of the efforts of William the dreamer to find where the abode is of Do-well, Do-bet, and Do-best. In fact, it is easy to point to the particular passage in the "Vision" which he was thinking of. The first fifteen lines of the Prologue to the Vita de Do-well give the key-note to the "Crede," and I therefore quote them here by way of illustration.

> þus I robed in russet · romed I aboute
> Al a somer sesoun · for to seche Dowel,
> And fraynide ful ofte · of folk þat I mette
> ȝif any wiȝt wiste · where Dowel was at inne,
> And what man he miȝte be · of many man I askide.
> Was neuer wiht as I wente · þat me wisse couþe
> Wher þis ladde loggede · lasse ne more ;
> Til hit fel on a Friday · twei Freres I mette,
> Maistres of þe Menours · men of grete wittes.
> Ich heilede hem hendeli · as ich hedde i-leorned,
> And preiede hem, par charite · er þei passede furre,
> "ȝif þei knewen any cuntre · or coostes aboute
> Wher þat Dowel dwelleþ · do me to wisse."
> "Mari," quod þe Menour · "among vs he dwelleþ,
> And euer haþ, as ich hope · and euer schal her-after."
>
> PIERS PLOWMAN, (ed. Skeat, 1867) ; *Text* A. ix. 1—15.

We should observe, too, that the two authors take rather different views of "Piers the Ploughman." Langland considers him as the type of a class of industrious and lowly-minded men, who guided their life by the Gospel, and by their influence induced others to admire and practise a pure and simple form of Christianity based upon a true-felt love for their fellows. Langland's Ploughman gives good advice even to the knight and to gentle ladies ; and, towards the end of the poem, he introduces *the* Piers Ploughman, *par excellence*, the good Samaritan above all others, Jesus Christ the righteous. But the Ploughman in the Crede is an individual, a ploughman and no more, described as in an abject state of poverty, yet so gifted with homely common sense as fully to see through all the tricks of the friars, and knowing very little more than is necessary for his soul's health, little more than the Creed and the Gospels. It is perhaps right to remind the reader that there is a difference even in the very *titles* of the poems. The one is "Piers Ploughman's Crede," i. e. the creed which the ploughman taught; the other is "Visio Willelmi de Petro Ploughman," the "Vision of Piers Ploughman which William saw," and which may be spoken of as the "Vision," or as "Piers Ploughman," but *never* as "Piers Ploughman's Vision," except by such as have no regard for accuracy, and who would not stick at using the term "Christian's Vision" as an equivalent one to Bunyan's vision of one Christian.

§ 13. Any further information about the author of the "Crede" can only be obtained by the discovery of other poems which he may have written. Now there are some poems printed in "Monumenta Franciscana," pp. 591—608, and again printed in Wright's "Political Poems," vol. i. pp. 253—270, which are worth some attention. The first is in Latin, the second two (of which Mr Brewer has made three) in English; they are all by the same author, and clearly written during the reign of Richard II.[1] by one who says that he had been a novice in the order of St Francis, but had left it to become a Wycliffite; also, that he was not an *apostata*, as he had not stayed in the convent his full year, but only about ten months and twenty days. They are outspoken attacks upon the friars, and upon the Minorites in particular, and at first sight seem to have a good deal in common with the "Crede." A careful scrutiny, however, of their language makes the identity of authorship seem doubtful, and, though it seemed to me at first probable, I now give it up; though, at the same time, these poems well deserve to be compared with the "Crede," and I have therefore quoted from them occasionally in the Notes. But there is another poem which stands a close scrutiny better, and deserves yet more attention, and this is no other than the well-known "Plowman's Tale," which has even been attributed to Chaucer, though it most certainly is not his. It may be found among the Canterbury Tales in most old editions subsequent to 1542; and also under the title of the "Complaint of the Ploughman," in Wright's "Political Poems," vol. i. pp. 304—346. Now the writer of this piece distinctly

---

[1] The one in Latin describes the council held at London in A.D. 1382.

claims to have written the "Crede;" for he says,

"Of freres I have told before
In a making of a Crede;"

i. e. in a poem named a "Creed." Mr Wright, if I interpret him correctly, seems to think this means no more than that the two poems were written by two men of the same way of thinking. But I am inclined to take it literally, simply in the plain sense which the words naturally bear. After reading this "Complaint of the Ploughman" again and again, I am more and more convinced that its writer states the simple truth. The dialect of the poems is the same; there is the same use of the past participle beginning with *I-* or *Y-*; the vocabulary is very similar; identities of phrase occur in many places; whilst the object of both is precisely the same, viz. to attack the friars, and to defend Wycliffe. The proof would be somewhat tedious from the very great number of similarities which might be adduced; but some of the most striking will be found in the notes. It is quite a noticeable feature in the "Crede" how frequently the words *glose, glosinge, glosed* occur; and there is precisely the same repetition of them in the "Complaint." In both poems occur such remarkable words as *tote* (to look), *angerliche, baselards, falshed, defended* (forbade), *bigge* (to build), *crochettes* or *crokettes, eggeth, fraitours, hernes, fain* (to feign), *sewe* (to follow), *queint, queintise* (in the peculiar sense of *crafty, craft*), *lorell, wisse, se* (seat), *curates, wilne, sain* (to say), *seker* or *siker, trusse* (to pack), *hongen* (to hang), and many others. The full force of the argument can only be perceived by a reader who compares the poems for himself, and consists even more in the fact that the *force* of the above words in both poems is generally the same, than in the mere occurrence of the words themselves; yet even this is of great weight, considering how short the poems are, and how rare are some of the words. Then again, we find, in both, like peculiar expressions such as, *curteis Christ, cutted clothes,* &c. But the similarities which a reader would probably attach most weight to are such as these which I here tabulate.

Quoted from "The Complaint."	*Quoted from the "Crede."*
Ipainted and portred.	.. portreid and paynt (l. 121).
	.. peynt & portred (l. 192).
Such that cannot say her Crede.	y can noh3t my Crede (8).
They nold nat demen after the face.	þei shulden nou3t after þe face · neuer þe folke demen (670).
In cattel catching is her comfort.	And also y sey couetise · catel to fongen (146).
Market-beaters, and medling make.	At marketts & miracles · we medleþ vs nevere (107).
The poor in spirite Crist gan blesse.	And alle pouere in gost · God himself blisseþ (521).
With double worsted well ydight.	Of double worstede y-dy3t (228).
Masters to be called defended he tho.	.. ben maysters i-called þat þe gentill Iesus . . . purly defended (574).
Had they ben out of religioun, They must have hanged at the plowe,	[but for the temptation of worldly wealth]
Threshing and diking from toun to toune.	þei schulden deluen & diggen · and dongen þe erþe (785).
They must have hanged at the plowe.	I sei3 a sely man me by · opon þe plow hongen (421).

Several more points of resemblance might be cited, but surely these are sufficient to confirm a statement made by the author himself, and *against* which there cannot be adduced any argument whatever. It may be looked upon, I think, as a proved fact; and I would ask the reader who has any lingering doubts fairly to compare the poems, and he will see how very much—to save space—I have understated and curtailed the proofs of it.

§ 14. There is no exact evidence for the date of the "Complaint," but Mr Wright puts it down at about 1393 or 1394, giving to the "Crede" the date 1392, and to the proceedings against Walter Brute that of 1391. But these proceedings lasted some time, and were not over till 1393, being merely *commenced* in 1391; and on this account

I assign about 1394 as the date of the "Crede," and about 1395 as that of the "Complaint." These dates satisfy every condition, and I do not think will ever need much alteration.

§ 15. The "Crede" has always been a favourite poem. Dr Whitaker quotes the following. "A piece" (says Mr Rawlinson, speaking of the CREDE) "rare and good, in which the remains of Monastic Antiquity are graphically describ'd. It charms me on that account when e'er I read it;" Hearne. MS. *Collections*, Vol. lxxxii. page 75. It has several passages of great interest, as for instance, the celebrated description (one of the best we have) of a Dominican convent. The pillars were painted and polished, and carved with curious knots. The windows were well wrought and lofty. The buildings were well walled-in all round, with postern-doors for easy egress. There were gardens and "erberes" (*herbaria*) with well-clipped borders, a cross curiously carved, and "tabernacles" used for reconnoitring from. Then there was the minster with its arches, and crockets, and knots of gold, its painted windows glorious with coats-of-arms and merchants' marks, its tombs with knights in alabaster, and lovely ladies by their side in gay garments; its cloisters pillared and painted, covered with lead and paved with painted tiles, with conduits of tin and lavers of "latun;" and its chapter-house fairly carved, and with a splendid ceiling. Then there was a refectory like a king's hall, regal kitchens, a dormitory with strong doors, halls, houses, chambers, infirmary, &c.; and then yet more houses with gay garrets, and every window-hole glased. How excellent, again, are the portraits of the fat friar with his double-chin shaking about, as big as a goose's egg, and the poor ploughman with his hood full of holes and his mittens made of patches, followed by his poor wife going "bare-foot on the bare ice, that the blood followed!" Whilst the cry of the ploughman's children sums up the early history of the poor of England in the words—

> "And alle þey songen o songe · þat sorwe was to heren;
> þey crieden alle o cry · a *carefull* note."

The real value of the poem lies, in fact, in these and other vivid and exact descriptions, which are alike useful to the antiquary and interesting to the general reader, as they give a clear insight into the condition of the poor, the animosity which existed between the friars and the secular clergy, and, most striking point of all, the utter contempt in which the orders held each other, and the audacity with which each tried to surpass the rest both in pitiless extortion and in proud display. To sum up all briefly, the poem is one which deserves not only to be read, but to be studied; it is one of those which is much more interesting on a second perusal than on a first, and continually improves upon acquaintance. It is well illustrated by, and well illustrates, Chaucer, and, in particular, the "Sompnoures Tale." It is of much value to lexicographers, who have made considerable use of it ; and it is on this account (as well as with a view to make this edition suitable for use in schools), that I have tried to make the Glossarial Index tolerably full and complete.[1]

§ 16. NOTE ON THE FIVE EXTRA LINES NOW FIRST PRINTED. It has been already mentioned that the MSS. are shewn to be independent of the printed edition by the appearance in them of five new lines. It so happens that these lines are certainly genuine, and of some importance. They are ll. 822, 823, and 828, 829, and 830. It is quite easy to see why Reynold Wolfe did not print them ; they savoured far too much of the doctrine of transubstantiation to be likely to be acceptable to Protestant readers in the reign of Edward VI. ; and he therefore purposely suppressed them. But he did it very clumsily, for he quite overlooked the fact that the omission of them took away the clue to the context and quite robbed it of all meaning, so that the whole of ll. 824—827 and 831—840 seem to be inserted, much to the reader's bewilderment, literally *à-propos* of nothing.[2] But now that these lines are restored, the drift of this whole passage is clear enough, and we perceive that the author is attacking the friars on yet one more point, viz. for the subtlety of their arguments about the sacrament of the mass, and for their attempts to explain a mystery which had much

---

[1] The word "Chapolory" is quoted in Richardson's Dictionary under the head of *Chapel*, by a strange blunder; and the word "Poynt-til," which is given in many dictionaries, is, I believe, one which never existed except by a misprint; see note to l. 194.

[2] He made yet another clumsy alteration; viz. by substituting "Abbot" for "bychop" in ll. 718 and 756, regardless of alliteration.

better, in his opinion, be left unexplained. His belief is, he says, that "God's body and blood are really in the sacrament; and though proud friars dispute about God's deity like dotards, the more the matter is stirred, the more confused they become. Christ said it *is* so; then what need of more words? No need to study and bestir our wits. These masters of divinity, many of them, do not follow the faith, as many of the common people do. How may any man's unassisted wit understand the mysteries of Christ that surpass all natural phenomena? A man must be of as meek a heart as Christ himself to receive the Holy Ghost by the purity of his life; and if a man is thus meek, he needs not to study the matter, nor to be called a Master (which Christ forbade), nor to put a cap on his bald pate; all he need do is to preach and live a pure life, and to use no pride." Such is the true sense of the whole passage, and it is quite consistent and intelligible. It appears further that, with some notion of hiding the omission, five lines, ll. 817—821, were inserted in the same edition; these I believe to be spurious, and of no older date than 1553. The imitation of style and spelling is very ingenious, but the alliteration in them is not so good. For further information, see note to l. 817, &c.

§ 17. GLOSSARY, &C. TO THE FIRST PRINTED EDITION. The edition of 1553 has some lines "to the reader" prefixed to it, and a Glossary at the end.[1] These are of little importance, but are printed here for completeness' sake. On the back of the title-page we find, in italics—

"*To the Reader.*
To read strange newes, desires manye,
 Which at my hande they can not haue ;
For here is but antiquitie
 Expressed only, as tholde booke gaue.
Take in good part, and not depraue
 The Ploughmans Crede, ientyll reader :
Loo, this is all that I requyer."

On the last leaf we find, in black letter—"For to occupie this leaffe which els shuld haue ben vacant, I haue made an interpretation of certayne hard wordes vsed in this booke for the better vnderstandyng of it.

[1] Also a few side-notes, printed in this volume in *capital letters*.

Frayning, forsakyng	Ey, egge
Wunede,[1] wont	Lellich, truely
Graith, truth	Egged, moued
Erde, erth	Theigh, though
Leue, beleue	Loresmen, learned men
God,[2] good	Stightle, stay
Byiapeth, deceiueth	Cherlich, gladly
Glaueryng, flattering	Louted, bowed
Puple, people	Preing,[8] praisyng
Cholede,[3] suffered	Fonden, walk
Glees, playes	Halt, kept
Hobelen, skipping	Hetes,[9] commaundements
Monelich,[4] monylesse	Sigge, say
Pulched, polished	Ho, she
Mightestou, mihgtest[5] thou	Rotheren, oxon
Semed,[6] gased	Dreccheth, drouneth
yerne, ofte	Lacchen, catchen
Queintly, strangely	Lakke, blame
Pure, very	Yerd,[10] rodde
Munte, went	Mystremen, nedy men
Bellich, well	Terre poughe, tar box
Tild, set	Pris liif, cheif or young
Hyrnes,[7] caues	Forgabbed, belyed
Feele, many	Waynen,[11] banysh

The residue the diligent reader shall (I trust) well ynough perceiue."

[1] Refers to l. 32, where the old printed *text* has *wennede*.
[2] Refers to l. 42, where Dr Whitaker thinks it means *God*, and I incline to think so too.
[3] *Sic;* an error for *Tholede*, l. 90.
[4] An error for *Menelich*, l. 108.
[5] *Sic.*
[6] An error for ʒemed, l. 159.
[7] See note to l. 182.
[8] The old *text* has *preying*, i. e. prayiug, l. 336.
[9] For *Hestes;* cf. l. 345 with l. 26.
[10] Only occurs in Lym-ʒerde, l. 564.
[11] *Sic;* an error for Wayuen. It should be noted that many of these explanations are quite wrong; see the Glossarial Index.

ADDITIONS AND CORRECTIONS.

P. iii, l. 2 *from bottom.* The British Museum MS. is on vellum.

P. 35, note to l. 65. The Pied Friars had but one house, viz. at Norwich. The order was dissolved, and they had to join one of the principal orders; we may infer that they joined the Carmelites.

P. 54, l. 782. Cf.
"But, Jak, thouȝ thi questions semen to thee wyse,
ȝet liȝtly a lewid man maye *leyen hem a water;*"
Reply of Frier Dawe Topias; *Pol. Poems,* ii. 43.

P. 73. The poem, with the burden "London," &c., is printed in Reliq. Antiq. i. 205. In l. 30 of God spede the Plough, "a styk of a bough" means a tally; see note to Piers Plowman, iv. 48.

L. 428. Mr Furnivall has kindly sent me the following quotation, which helps to shew that the meaning of *mete* is scanty or insufficient, in the present passage.

"'Ile cloth my-selfe in strange array,
in a beggars habbitt I will goe.'...
John, hee gott on a *clouted* cloake,
soe *meete* & low then by his knee," &c.
William Stewart and John; Bp. Percy's Folio MS., p. 432.

L. 627. With regard to ll. 627-629, a reply to my query in "Notes and Queries" has appeared, written by Mr G. A. Sala. See N. & Q., 3rd S. xii. 211.

GLOSSARY.

Cloutede, patched; perhaps without reference to the *cleat;* see Gloss. to Will. of Palerne.

Hokschynes, gaiters, 426. Compare the Ayrshire *hoeshins* or *hushions,* Ross. *hoggers;* another form of *hoskins,* the dimin. of *hose.* The *hoeshins* are of various sorts; some are made of old stockings with the feet cut off. For the change of *ks* and *sk,* cf. *axe* with *ask.*

"Mete" means scanty, insufficient; see the note to l. 428, and compare the following quotation, sent me by Mr Wedgwood—
"There's no room at my side, Margaret,
My coffin's made so *meet.*"

Add—Starep, sparkle, shine, 553. Wayten, look out, watch, 469.

Peres the Ploughmans Crede.

Cros, and Curteis Crist · þis begynnynge spede,   *Christ and His cross speed this beginning!*
For þe faderes frendchipe · þat fourmede Heuene,
And þoruȝ þe speciall spirit · þat sprong of hem tweyne,
And alle in on godhed · endles dwelleþ!   4
A and all myn A.b.c · after haue y lerned,   *I know my Paternoster and my Ave, but I know not yet my Creed.*
And [patred] in my *pater-noster* · iche poynt after oþer,
And after all, myn *Aue-marie* · almost to þe ende ;   7
But all my kare is to comen · for y can nohȝt my Crede.
Whan y schal schewen myn schrift · schent mote y worþen,
þe prest wil me punyche · & penaunce enioyne ;
þe Lengþe of a Lenten · flech moot y leue   *I shall have to fast 40 days after Easter is come.*
After þat Estur ys ycomen · and þat is hard fare ;   12
And Wedenes-day iche wyke · wiþ-outen flech-mete.
And also Jesu hym-self · to the Jewes he seyde,
"He þat leeueþ nouȝt on me · he leseþ þe blisse."
þerfor lerne þe byleue · leuest me were,   16   *Therefore must I learn my Creed, if any true man will teach me.*
And if any werldly wiȝt · wille me couþe,
Oþer lewed or lered · þat lyueþ þerafter,
And fulliche folweth þe feyþ · and feyneþ non oþer ;
þat no worldliche wele · wilneþ no tyme,   20
But lyueþ in louynge of God · and his lawe holdeþ,
And for no getynge of good · neuer his God greueþ,

---

3. *spirit*] sprite B.
6. [*patred*] patres AC; partes B; see note, and footnote to l. 451.
8. For y, A *has* þ *by mistake, here and in* l. 9; BC *have* I.
17. *And if*] Yf B; Gif C.
19. *feyþ*] feyȝ A; Faithe B; feith C; *cf.* l. 95.
20. *wilneþ—tyme*] willeth at no tyme (*over an erasure*) B.

But follow[e]þ him þe full wey · as he þe folke taughte.

I question many men, but they cannot tell me.

But to many maner of men · þis matter is asked, 24
Boþe to lered and to lewed · þat seyn þat þey leueden
Hollich on þe grete god · and holden alle his hestes;
But by a fraynyng for-þan · faileþ þer manye. 27

First I asked the Friars, who said the lock of belief lay locked in their hands.

For first y fraynede þe freres · and þey me fulle tolden,
þat all þe frute of þe fayþ · was in here foure ordres,
And þe cofres of cristendam · & þe keye boþen,
And þe lok [of beleve · lyeth] loken in her hondes.

MINORITES, OR GRAYE FRERES. I asked a Minorite first,

Þanne [wende] y to wyten · & wiþ a whiȝt y mette, 32
A Menoure in a morow-tide · & to þis man I saide,
"Sire, for grete god[e]s loue · þe graiþ þou me telle,
Of what myddelerde man · myȝte y best lerne
My Crede? For I can it nouȝt · my kare is þe more; 36
& þerfore, for Cristes loue! · þi councell y praie.

telling him that I thought a Carmelite could teach me.

A Carm me haþ y-couenaunt · þe Crede me to teche;
But for þou knowest Carmes well · þi counsaile y aske."

The Minorite thought me mad, and said,

Þis Menour loked on me · and lawȝyng he seyde, 40
"Leue Cristen man · y leue þat þou madde!
Whouȝ schulde þei techen þe God · þat con not hemselue?

"Carmelites are mere jugglers, and jesters by nature,

Þei ben but jugulers · and iapers, of kynde,
Lorels and Lechures · & lemmans holden; 44
Neyþer in order ne out · but vn-neþe lybbeþ,
And byiapeþ þe folke · wiþ gestes of Rome!
It is but a faynt folk · i-founded vp-on iapes,

---

23. *followeþ*] followþ A; Followith B; folweth C.
25. *þey*] A *has* þeþ *by mistake, here and in* l. 28; BC *have* they. *leueden*] leveden B; liueden C.
26. *hestes*] hesteg (*sic*) A; hestys B; hestes C.
27. *fraynyng*] fraþnyng A; fraynyng BC.
28. *freres*] Friers B. *þey me fulle*] them full B (*where the* m *is over an erasure*).
30. *boþen*] beþen A; bethen (?) B; bothen C.

31. [*of—lyeth*] *From* B; of byleue lieth C; an lene his A (*corruptly*).
32. [*wende*] wend B; wennede C; wittede A. *wyten*] wytten C.
33. *Menoure*] Minoure C.
34. *godes*] gods A; godes BC. *graiþ*] graith C; truith (*over* graith *erased*) B.
38. *Crede*] *So in* AB; C *has* nede.*
40. *Menour*] mynour B; Minour C.
41. *þat—madde*] that thou maid B; that thou madde C; *see* l. 280.
42. *schulde*] *miswritten* schude *in* A.
43. *jugulers*] ÿugulers A; iugulers C.
46. *gestes*] iestes B.

þei makeþ hem Maries men · (so þei men tellen), 48   *who lie about our Lady, and betray women.*
And lieþ on our Ladie · many a longe tale.
And þat wicked folke · wymmen bi-traieþ,
And bigileþ hem of her good · wiþ glauerynge wordes,
And þerwiþ holden her hous · in harlotes werkes. 52
And, so saue me God! · I hold it gret synne   *It is a great sin to give them anything.*
To ȝyuen hem any good · swiche glotones to fynde,
To maynteyne swiche¹ maner men · þat mychel good   [¹ MS. "swicle."]
  destruyeþ.
Ȝet seyn they in here sutilte · to sottes in townes, 56
Þei comen out of Carmeli · Crist for to followen,
& feyneþ hem with holynes · þat yuele hem bisemeþ.
Þei lyuen more in lecherie · and lieth in her tales   *They live more in lechery than in good life; which they would not do, if they knew their Creed.*
þan suen any god liife; · but [lurken] in her selles, 60
[And] wynnen werldliche god · & wasten it in synne.
And ȝif þei couþen her crede · oþer on Crist leueden,
þei weren nouȝt so hardie · swich harlotri vsen.
Sikerli y can nouȝt fynden · who hem first founded, 64   *No one founded these Piedfriars; they founded themselves.*
But þe foles foundeden hem-self · freres of the Pye,
And maken hem mendynauns · & marre þe puple.
But what glut of þo gomes · may any good kachen,   *Every glutton among them keeps all to himself.*
He will kepen it hym-self · & cofren it faste, 68
And þeiȝ his felawes fayle good · for him he may
  steruen.
Her money may bi-quest · & testament maken,   *People may leave them money, and then do as they like.*
And no obedience bere · but don as [hem] luste.
[And] ryȝt as Robertes men · raken aboute, 72
At feires & at ful ales · & fyllen þe cuppe,   *They loaf about at fairs.*
And precheþ all of pardon · to plesen the puple.

48. *so*] and so BC.
49. *lieþ*] leyth B; leieth C.
53. *gret*] great B; greate C.
57. *followen*] folwen C.
59. *lyuen*] leyvin B.   *tales*] tallys B.
60. *suen*] schewin B.   [*lurken* C] *lyrken* A; lurkyn B.
61. [*And*] But ABC.   *werldliche*]

werdliche C.
62. *ȝif*] Yef B; ghif C.
65. *foundeden*] Foundon B.
68. *hymself*] hem self C.
69. *þeiȝ*] though B; thoigh C.
71. *no*] none BC. [*hem*] hym ABC (*wrongly*).   *luste*] list B.
72. [*And*] so in BC; A *has* tryȝt = & ryȝt; *see l.* 215.

1 *

4   LUXURY OF THE CARMELITES.

              Her pacience is all pased · & put out to ferme,
              And pride is in her pouerte · þat litell is to preisen. 76
              And at þe lulling of oure Ladye · þe wymmen to lyken,

They are great at Miracle-plays.   And miracles of mydwyves · & maken wymmen to wenen
              þat þe lace of oure ladie smok · liȝteþ hem of children.
              þei ne prechen nouȝt of Powel · ne penaunce for synne,
              But all of mercy & mensk · þat Marie maie helpen. 81

They follow after women, whom they call their sisters.   Wiþ sterne staues and stronge · þey ouer lond strakeþ
              þider as her lemmans liggeþ · and lurkeþ in townes,
              (Grey grete-hedede quenes · wiþ gold by þe eiȝen), 84
              And seyn, þat here sustren þei ben · þat soiourneþ
                 aboute ;
              And þus about þey gon · & godes folke by-traieþ.

St Paul preached about such as these; Phil. iii. 18, 19.   It is þe puple þat Powel · preched of in his tyme ;
              He seyde of swich folk · þat so aboute wente,   88
              'Wepyng, y warne ȝow · of walkers aboute ;
              It beþ enemyes of þe cros · þat crist opon polede.
              Swiche slomerers in slepe · slauþe is her ende,
              And glotony is her God · wiþ g[l]oppyng of drynk, 92
              And gladnes in glees · & gret ioye y-maked ;
              In þe schendyng of swiche · schall mychel folk lawȝe.'

So don't believe them, my friend, but let them go!"   þerfore, frend, for þi feyþ · fond to don betere,
              Leue nouȝt on þo losels · but let hem forþ pasen,   96
              For þei ben fals in her feiþ · & fele mo oþere."

"But can you not tell me of any one who can teach me my Creed?"   "Alas ! frere," quaþ I þo · "my purpos is i-failed,
              Now is my counfort a-cast ! · canstou no bote,
              Where y myȝte meten wiþ a man · þat myȝte me
                 [wissen]   100
              For to conne my Crede · Crist for to folwen ?"

80. *Powel*] Pawle B.
81. *mercí—mensk*] mary and melk (!) B.
84. *eiȝen*] eighen C.
85. *sustren*] sustern C.
87. *Powel* C] Powell A ; Powle B.
89. *ȝow*] you BC.
90. *opon*] vpon BC. *polede*] tho lede C.

91. *slomerers*] slomrers C. *slauþe*] slauth B ; slaughte C. *her*] ther B.
92. *gloppyng*] goppyng A ; golping B ; gloppynge C.
94. *mychel folk*] many B.
95. *fond*] Found B.
99. *counfort*] comfort BC.
100. [*wissen*] wyssen C ; willen A (*by mistake for* wiflen); whiffen B.

"CERTEYNE, felawe," quaþ þe frere · "wiþ-outen any *Minorites.*
faile. *"Certainly, yes."*

Of all men opon mold · we Menures most scheweþ *We Minorites lead*
þe pure Apostell[e]s life · wiþ penance on erþe, 104 *the most holy life.*
And suen hem in saunctite · & suffren well harde.
We haunten none tauernes · ne hobelen abouten; *We haunt no*
At marketts & myracles · we medleþ vs nevere; *taverns, or markets, or plays.*
We hondlen no money · but menelich faren, 108
And haven hunger at [the] meate · at ich a mel ones.
We hauen forsaken the worlde · & in wo lybbeþ,
In penaunce & pouerte · & precheþ þe puple, *We live in poverty, and pray*
By ensample of oure life · soules to helpen; 112 *for all our lay brethren who give*
And in pouertie praien · for all oure parteners *us anything.*
þat ʒyueþ vs any good · god to honouren,
Oþer bell oþer booke · or breed to our fode,
Oþer catell oþer cloþ · to coveren wiþ our bones, 116
Money or money-worthe; · here mede is in heven.
For we buldeþ a burwʒ · a brod and a large, *For we build a large convent,*
A Chirche and A Chapaile · with chambers a-lofte, *with windows and high walls.*
Wiþ wide windowes y-wrouʒt · & walles well heye, 120
þat mote bene portreid and paynt · & pulched ful clene,
Wiþ gaie glittering glas · glowing as þe sonne.
And myʒtestou amenden vs · wiþ money of þyn owne, *Only give us something, and*
þou chuldest enely bifore Crist · in compas of gold 124 *you shall be painted in our*
In þe wide windowe westwarde · wel niʒe in the myddell, *west window,*
And seynt Fraunces him-self · schall folden the in his *kneeling before Christ.*
cope,
And presente the to the trynitie · and praie for thy
synnes;

103. *opon*] vpon C. *Menures*] menniers B; Minorites C.
104. *Apostelles*] Apostells A; aposteles C; apostylles B.
106. *none*] no C.
107. *medeleþ*] medeley *C.
108. *menelich*] monelich *C.
109. [*the* BC] þer A (*wrongly*).
110. *lybbeth*] *resembles* lyvveth *in* A.
117. *or*] other BC.
119. *Chapaile*] chapitre B (*over an erasure*); chapitle C.
121. *paynt*] payntyd B; paint C.
123. *owne*] owen C.
124. *chuldest enely*] chouldest knely C; shouldest knely B.
125. *windowe*] wyndowes B; window C.

Your name shall be read there for ever.	þi name schall noblich ben wryten · & wrouȝt for the nones, 128
	And, in remembrance of þe · y-rade þer for euer.
	And, broþer, be þou nouȝt aferd; · [bythenk in] thyn herte,
Never mind your Creed; I can easily assoil you."	Houȝ þou conne nouȝt þi Crede · kare þou no more.
	I schal asoilen þe, syre · & setten it on my soule, 132
	And þou maie maken þis good · þenk þou non oþer."
	"SIRE," y saide, "in certaine · y schal gon & asaye;"—
I promised to try and find him something; he assoiled me, and I left him.	And he sette on me his honde · & asoilede me clene,
	And þeir y parted him fro · wiþ-outen any peine, 136
	In couenant þat y come aȝen · Crist he me be-tauȝte.
	Þanne suide y to my-self · " here semeþ litel trewþe !
Then I thought of Christ's words (Mat. vii. 1-4);	First to blamen his broþer · and bacbyten him foule,
	Þeire-as curteis Crist · clereliche saide, 140
	'Whow myȝt-tou in thine broþer eiȝe · a bare mote loken,
	And in þyn owen eiȝe · nouȝt a bem toten ?
	See fyrst on þi-self · and siþen on anoþer,
	And clense clene þi syȝt · and kepe well þyn eiȝe, 144
	And for anoþer mannes eiȝe · ordeyne after.'
and how he blamed covetousness (Luke xii. 15);	And also y sey coueitise · catel to fongen,
	Þat Crist haþ clerliche forboden · & clenliche destruede,
	And saide to his sueres · forsoþe on þis wise, 148
	' Nouȝt þi neiȝbours good · couet yn no tyme.'
	But charite & chastete · ben chased out clene,
and that men are known by their fruits (Mat. vii. 20).	But Crist seide, ' by her fruyt · men shall hem ful knowen.' " 151
	Þanne saide y, " certeyn, sire · þou demest full trewe !"

128. *noblich*] *So in* BC; A *really has* nobliþ, *a mistake caused by reading* noblich *as* noblith.
130. [*bythenk in*] *So in* C; A *corruptly has* by þenken.
134. *gon*] *So in* BC; A *has* gone.
137. *betauȝte*] A *really has* betaiȝte (*with the* i *undotted*) *by mere mistake;* betaught BC.
141. *myȝttou*] myght thou BC. *thine*] thy C. *broþer*] brothers C.
146. *sey*] saye B; see C.
147. *destruede*] distrayid B; destruedē C.
149. *couet yn*] couetyn A; coveit not at B; coueyte in C.

Þanne þouʒt y to frayne þe first · of þis foure ordirs,   *I determined to try the Dominicans.*
And presede to þe prechoures · to proven here wille.
[Ich] hiʒede to her house · to herken of more;
And whan y cam to þat court · y gaped aboute.   156
Swich a bild bold, y-buld · opon erþe heiʒte   *I had never seen such a building as their convent.*
Say i nouʒt in certeine · siþþe a longe tyme.
Y ʒemede vpon þat house · & ʒerne þeron loked,   159
Whouʒ þe pileres weren y-peynt · and pulched ful clene,   *It had painted and polished pillars,*
And queynteli i-corven · wiþ curiouse knottes,
Wiþ wyndowes well y-wrouʒt · wide vp o-lofte.   *wide windows,*
And þanne y entrid in · and even-forþ went,
And all was walled þat wone · þouʒ it wid were,   164
Wiþ posternes in pryuytie · to pasen when hem liste;   *privy posterns, orchards, and gardens.*
Orcheʒardes and erberes · euesed well clene,
And a curious cros · craftly entayled,
Wiþ tabernacles y-tiʒt · to toten all abouten.   168
Þe pris of a plouʒ-lond · of penyes so rounde
To aparaile þat pyler · were pure lytel.
Þanne y munte me forþ · þe mynstre to knowen,   *The minster was well built,*
And a-waytede a woon · wonderlie well y-beld,   172
Wiþ arches on eueriche half · & belliche y-corven,
Wiþ crochetes on corners · wiþ knottes of golde,   *with crockets and knots of gold,*
Wyde wyndowes y-wrouʒt · y-written full þikke,
Schynen wiþ schapen scheldes · to schewen aboute,   176
Wiþ merkes of marchauntes · y-medled bytwene,   *wide windows with coats-of-arms,*
Mo þan twenty and two · twyes y-noumbred.
Þer is none heraud þat haþ · halt swich a rolle,
Riʒt as a rageman · haþ rekned hem newe.   180
Tombes opon tabernacles · tyld opon lofte,   *and raised tombs of alabaster and marble,*
Housed in hirnes · harde set abouten,

155. [*Ich* C] With A (*by evident mistake*); ytche B.
157. *opon*] vpon C.
158. *Say*] Sawe B.
159. *ʒemede*] ʒemyd B; semed *C. *vpon*] apon B; opon C.
160. *Whouʒ*] How B; Whow C.
162. *ofofte*] aloft B; alofte C.
166. *Orcheʒardes*] Orcheyardes C; Orchardes B. *erberes*] Erbars B. *euesed* AC] vsyd B.
171. *munte*] mount B.
172. *a woon*] it anon (*over an erasure*) B; *cf. l.* 164. *ybeld*] ybild C.
181. *opon*] vpon C.
182. *hirnes*] hernis B; hornes *C.

                        Of armede alabaustre · clad for þe nones,
                        [Made vpon marbel · in many maner wyse,   184
*whereon lay   Knyghtes in her conisantes · clad for þe nones,]
sculptured
knights, with   All it semed seyntes · y-sacred opon erþe ;
lovely ladies
beside them.*   And louely ladies y-wrouʒt · leyen by her sydes
                        In many gay garmentes · þat weren gold-beten.   188
                        þouʒ þe tax of ten ʒer · were trewly y-gadered,
                        Nolde it nouʒt maken þat hous · half, as y trowe.
*The cloister was   þanne kam I to þat cloister · & gaped abouten   191
pillared and
painted, covered   Whouʒ it was pilered and peynt · & portred well clene,
with lead, and
paved with   All y-hyled wiþ leed · lowe to þe stones,
painted tiles.*
                        And y-paued wiþ peynt til · iche poynte after oþer ;
                        Wiþ kundites of clene tyn · closed all aboute,
                        Wiþ lauoures of latun · louelyche y-greithed.   196
                        I trowe þe gaynage of þe ground · in a gret schire
                        Nolde aparaile þat place · oo poynt til other ende.
*The chapter-house   þanne was þe chaptire-hous wrouʒt · as a greet chirche,
was carved and
sculptured, with a   Coruen and couered · and queyntliche entayled ;   200
fine ceiling.*
                        Wiþ semlich selure · y-set on lofte ;
                        As a Parlement-hous · y-peynted aboute.
*The refectory was   þanne ferd y into fraytour · and fond þere an oþer, 203
like a royal hall,
and glazed like a   An halle for an heyʒ kinge · an housholde to holden,
church.*
                        Wiþ brode bordes aboute · y-benched wel clene,
                        Wiþ windowes of glas · wrouʒt as a Chirche.
                        þanne walkede y ferrer · & went all abouten,
                        And seiʒ halles full hyʒe · & houses full noble, 208
*There were other   Chambers wiþ chymneyes · & Chapells gaie ;
chambers, and
chapels, and*   And kychens for an hyʒe kinge · in castells to holden,

184, 185. *Omitted in* A ; *I give these lines from* B, *only altering* yᵉ nonys *into* þe nones, *and* Knytes *into* Knyghtes.
184. *vpon*] opon C.
185. *her conisantes,*] ther conisante C.
187. *leyen*] lyen B.
188. *garmentes*] garnemens C.
192. *portred*] porteryd B ; portreyd C.

194. *peynt til*] painetyle B (*indistinct, and with some letter written over* paine) ; poynttyl C.
199. *chaptire*] chapter B ; chapitre C.
201. *yset*] yseet *C; I-sett B.
206. *glas*] glase B ; glaas C.
208. *seiʒ*] seigh C ; see B.
209. *chymneyes*] chymneys C chymbneis B.

And her dortour y-di3te · wiþ dores ful stronge ;   *kitchens; also a*
Formery and fraitur · with fele mo houses,   212 *dormitory and infirmary with a refectory.*
And all strong ston wall · sterne opon heiþe,
Wiþ gaie garites & grete · & iche hole y-glased ;
[*And oþere*] houses y-nowe · to herberwe þe queene. *Yet will these builders beg a*
And 3et þise bilderes wilne beggen · a bagg-ful of   *bagful of wheat of any man however*
   wheate   216 *poor.*
Of a pure pore man · þat maie oneþe paie
Half his rente in a 3er · and half ben behynde !
Þanne turned y a3en · whan y hadde all y-toted,
And fond in a freitour · a frere on a benche,   220 *I found in a refectory a friar*
A greet cherl & a grym · growen as a tonne,   *on a bench, with fat face,*
Wiþ a face as fat · as a full bledder,
Blowen bretfull of breþ · & as a bagge honged   223
On boþen his chekes, & his chyn · wiþ a chol lollede, *and a double-chin big as a goose's*
As greet as a gos eye · growen all of grece ;   *egg.*
Þat all wagged his fleche · as a quyk myre.
His cope þat biclypped him · wel clene was it folden, *His cope was of doubled worsted,*
Of double worstede y-dy3t · doun to þe hele ;   228 *and his kirtle clean white.*
His kyrtel of clene whijt · clenlyche y-sewed ;
Hyt was good y-now of ground · greyn for to beren.
I haylsede þat herdeman · & hendliche y saide,
"Gode syre, for Godes loue · canstou me graiþ tellen 233
To any worþely wij3t · þat [wissen] me couþe
Whou y schulde conne my Crede · Crist for to folowe, *I prayed him to tell me of one who*
Þat leuede lelliche him-self · & lyuede þerafter,   *could teach me my Creed.*
Þat feynede non falshede · but fully Crist suwede ? 236
For sich a certeyn man · syker wold y trosten,
Þat he wolde telle me þe trewþe · and turne to none
   oþer.   *"An Austin*
And an Austyn þis ender daie · egged me faste ;   239 *friar," said I,*

215. [*And oþere*] A *has to þere, by mistake for* & *oþere;* BC *have* And other. *Cf. footnote to l.* 72.
217. *pure*] B *omits*.
221. *cherl*] chorl C.
222. *as fat as*] so fat as C.
224. *a chol*] achole B.
225. *As*] So C. *gos eye*] gose egg B. *all*] ffull (*over an erasure*) B.
233. [*wissen*] willen A; wiffen B; wissen C; *see l.* 100.
235. *leuede*] levid B; lenede *C.
236. *non*] no C.
237. *trosten*] tresten B.

"told me his order was first founded."	þat he wolde techen me wel · he plyȝt me his treuþe,
	And seyde me, 'serteyne · syþen Crist died
	Oure ordir was [euelles] · & erst y-founde.'"
"First!" said he, "he is a mere abortion!"	"Fyrst, felawe!" quaþ he · "fy on his pilche! He is but abortijf · eked wiþ cloutes! 244
	He holdeþ his ordynaunce · wiþe hores and þeues,
	And purchaseþ hem pryuileges · wiþ penyes so rounde;
	It is a pur pardoners craft · proue & asaye!
	For haue þei þi money · a moneþ þerafter, 248
	Certes, þeiȝ þou come aȝen · he nyl þe nouȝt knowen.
Ours was the one first founded, and we are the best approved clerks.	But, felawe, our foundement · was first of þe oþere, And we ben founded fulliche · wiþ-outen fayntise; And we ben clerkes y-cnowen · cunnynge in scole, 252
	Proued in procession · by processe of lawe.
	Of oure ordre þer beþ · bichopes wel mauye,
	Scyntes on sundry stedes · þat suffreden harde;
We can be popes; we are of highest degree."	And we ben proued þe prijs · of popes at Rome, 256 And of gretest degre · as godspelles telleþ."
	"A! syre," quaþ y þanne · "þou seyst a gret wonder,
"Christ spake not thus," said I. Mat. xx. 26, 27;	Siþen Crist seyd hym-self · to all his disciples, 'Which of ȝou þat is most · most schal he werche, 260
	And who is goer byforne · first schal he seruen.'
Lu. x. 18.	And seyde, 'he sawe satan · sytten full heyȝe
	And ful lowe ben y-leyd;' · in lyknes he tolde,
	þat in pouernesse of spyrit · is spedfullest hele, 264
	And hertes of heynesse · harmeþ þe soule.
I bade him farewell, and left him.	And þerfore, frere, fare well · here fynde y but pride; Y preise nouȝt þi preching · but as a pure myte."
	And augerl[l]ich y wandrede · þe Austyns to proue, 268
The Augustine Freres. Then I found an	And mette wiþ a maister of þo men · & meklich y seyde, "Maister, for þe moder loue · þat Marie men kalleþ,

241. *syþen*] *miswritten* syȝen *in* A, *by mere slip;* sythyn B; syghthen C.
242. [*euelles*] *From* C; yvellis B; y-uelles (*altered to* y-ueffes) A.
248. *þi*] thy C; the B.
249. *nyl*] nyll B; wil C.
251. *byforne*] aforn B.

263. *ful lowe*] fullowe AB; fullow C (*but the words should be separated*).
265. *heynesse*] highnes (*also* heynesse *in margin*) B; heyne *C.
267. *preching*] prechyns *C.
268. *angerlich*] angreiche B, angerich AC; *see note*.

Knowest þou ouȝt, þer þou comest · a creatour on erþe,   *Austin friar, and asked where I could learn my Creed.*
þat coude me my Crede teche · and trewliche enſourme,
Wiþ-outen flaterynge fare · & noþing feyne ?   273
þat folweþ fulliche þe feiþ · and none other fables,
Wiþ-outen gabbynge of glose · as þe godspelles telleþ ?
A Menour haþ me holly by-hyȝt · to helen my soule,   *"A Minorite," said I, "will heal my soul,*
For he seiþ þat her sekte · is sykerest on erþe,   277
And ben kepers of þe keye · þat Cristendome helpeþ,   *for they keep the keys of Christendom."*
And pur[l]iche in pouerte · þe apostells þey suweþ."
"ALAS !" quaþ þe frier · " almost y madde in mynde,   *"Alas!" said he, "how these Minorites beguile men!*
To sen houȝ þis Minoures · many men begyleth !
Soþli, somme of þo gomes · haþ more good him-selue
þan ten knyȝtes þat y knowe · of catell in cofers !
In fraytour þei faren best · of all þe foure orders,   284
And [vsen] ypocricie · in all þat þey werchen,
And prechen all of parfitnes · but loke now, y þe praye,
Nouȝt but profre hem in pryvite · a [peny] for a masse,   *Only offer one a penny, and see if his man is ready to take it!*
And, but his cnaue be prest · put out myne eiȝe,   288
þouȝ he hadde more money hid · þan marchantes of wolle !
Loke houȝ þis loresmen · lordes bytrayen,
Seyn þat þey folwen fully · Fraunceses rewle,
þat in cotynge of his cope · is more cloþ y-folden   292
þan was in Fraunces froc · whan he hem first made.   *See what large copes they have, and yet they have a furred coat beneath; cut short though, so as not to be seen.*
And ȝet, vnder þat cope · a cote haþ he furred,
Wiþ foyns, or wiþ fitchewes · oþer fyn beuer,
And þat is cutted to þe kne · & queyntly y-botend, 296
Lest any spirituall man · aspie þat gile.
Fraunces bad his breþeren · barfote to wenden ; *They ought to go*

271. *creatour*] creature C.
273. *feyne*] fayne B.
275. *gabbynge*] gabynge C; gabbing B. *godspelles*] gospelles B.
276. *Menour*] minour B; Minoure C.
279. *purliche*] puriche ABC; *but see l.* 318.
283. *cofers*] cofres C.
285. [*vsen*] vsun C; vson B;

vsune A.
286. *all of*] of all B.
287. [*pcny* BC] pany A.
288. *cnaue*] knaue B; name *C. *prest*] Prest *C.
294. *haþ*] A *has* haþe (*badly*); hath BC.
295. *fitchewes*] fichewes C; ficheu B.

PRAISES OF THE AUGUSTINE FRIARS.

barefoot, and they have buckled shoes, and hose slily cut short.

Nou han þei bucled schon · for bleynynge of her heles,
And hosen in harde weder · y-hamled by þe ancle, 300
And spicerie sprad in her purse · to parten where hem lust.

Lords love them, for they seem so humble, but they are pure hypocrites.

Lordes loueth hem well · for þei so lowe crouchen;
But knewen men her cautel · & her queynt wordes,
Þei wolde worchypen hem · nouȝt but a litel, 304
Þe image of ypocricie · ymped vpon fendes.
But, sone, ȝif þou wilte ben syker · seche þou no ferther,

We were founded first, and were hermits in the wilderness,

We friers be þe first · and founded vpon treuþe.
Paul *primus* [*heremita*] · put vs him-selue 308
Awey into wildernes · þe werlde to dispisen;
And þere we leng[e]den full longe · & lyueden full harde,

till those friars invaded the towns,

For-to all þis freren folke · weren founded in townes,
And tauȝten vntrulie; · and þat we well aspiede, 312
And for chefe charitie · we chargeden vs seluen;
In amending of þis men · we maden oure celles

and we followed them, to amend them.

To ben in cyties y-set · to styȝtle þe people,
Preching & praying · as profetes schulden; 316
And so we holden vs þe heued · of all holy chirche.
We haue power of the pope · purliche assoilen

All that help our house we at once assoil.

All þat helpen our hous · in helpe of her soules,
To dispensen hem wiþ · in dedes of synne; 320
All þat amendeth oure hous · in money oþer elles,
Wiþ corne oþer catell · or cloþes of beddes,
Oþer bedys or broche · or breed for our fode.
And ȝif þou hast any good · & wilt þi-selfe helpen, 324

Do you help us, and we'll grant you a provincial

Helpe vs hertliche þerwiþe · & here I vndertake,
Þou schalt ben broþer of our hous · & a boke habben

---

299. *bleynynge*] bleynyng B; blen-
ynge C.
300. *yhamled*] y-hamelid B.
301. *sprad*] speed B.
303. *knewen*] knowen *C. *her*] A
wrongly has heir *the second time.*
307. *be*] beth C; bethe B.
308. [*heremita*] heremite ABC
(*wrongly*); *see note.*

310. *lengeden*] *So in* C; lengden
A; longeden B. *lyueden*] leueden C.
315. *styȝtle*] stightlen B; styghtle
C.
317. *heued*] hedd B (*over erasure*);
hetheued *C.
320. *hem wiþ*] with hem B.
322. *oþer*] or with B. *of*] to BC.

(At þe next chaptire) · clereliche enscaled ;   *letter; I'll assoil you now."*
And þanne oure prouinciall · haþ power to assoilen 328
Alle sustren & breþeren · þat beþ of our order.
And þou3 þou conne nou3t þi Crede · knele downe here ;
My soule y sette for þyn · to asoile þe clene,
In Couenaunt þat þou come againe · & katell vs
   bringe."   332
And þanne loutede y adoun · & he me leue grauntede,   *I knelt down, he assoiled me, and I left him,*
And so I partid him fro · & þe frere left.
Þanne seid I to my-self · " here is no bote ;   335
Heere pride is þe *pater-noster* · in preyinge of synne ;
Here Crede is coueytise ; · now can y no ferþer,   *to go to the Carmelites.*
3et will y fonden forþ · & fraynen þe Karmes."

Þ ANNE totede y into a tauerne · & þer y aspyede   *THE CARMELITES, OR WHYTE*
   Two frere Karmes · wiþ a full coppe.   340 *FRERES.*
Þere y auntrede me in · & ai[s]liche y seide,
" Leue syre, for þe lordes loue · þat þou on leuest,   *Seeing two Carmelites, I asked if either could help me to learn the Creed.*
Lere me to som man · my Crede for to lerne,
Þat lyueþ in [lel] lijf · and loueþ no synne,   344
And gloseþ nou3t þe godspell · but halt Godes he[s]tes,
And neþer money ne mede · ne may him nou3t letten
But werchen after Godes worde · wiþ-outen any faile.
A prechour y-professed · haþ pli3t me his trewþe   348 *"A Dominican," I said, " had offered to teach me truly."*
To techen me trewlie ; · but woldest þou me tellen
For þei ben certayne men · & syker on to trosten,
Y wolde quyten þe þi mede · as my mi3te were."

" A TROFLE," quaþ he, " trewlie ! · his treuþ is full
   litell !   352
He dyned nou3t wiþ Domynike · siþe Crist deide !   *" They are the princes of pride,"*
For wiþ þe princes of pride · þe prechours dwellen ;

---

827. *chaptire*] chapiter B; chapitre C.
   329. *sustren—breþeren*] susterne and brotherin B.
   336. *preyinge*] proyng B.
   338. *forþ*] fourth B.
   341. *auntrede*] aventeryd B. *ais-*
liche] aillich B ; aisliche C ; *see* note.
   343. *Lere*] teache (*over erasure*) B.
   344. [*lel* C] Lei A ; leele B.
   345. *hestes*] *In* A *and* C *miswritten* hetes; *but* B *has* hestys.
   352. A *has* trofle, *correctly* ; C *has* trefle.

said one, "and live with lords.	þei bene as digne as þe devel · þat droppeþ fro heuene.
	Wiþ hertes of heynesse · wouȝ halwen þei chirches 356
	And deleþ in devynitie · as dogges doþ bones!
	þei medleth wiþ messages · & mariages of grete;
	þey leeuen wiþ lordes · wiþ lesynges y-nowe;
	þey biggeþ hem bichopryches · wiþ bagges of golde; 360
	þei wilneþ worchipes— · but waite on her dedes!
Note their goings-on at Hertford,	Herken at Herdforþe · hou þat þey werchen,
	And loke whou þat þei lyven · & leeue as þou fyndest.
	þey [ben] counseilours of kinges · Crist wot þe soþe, 364
how they flatter the king.	Whou þey [curry] kinges · & her back claweþ!
	God leue hem leden well · in lyvinge of heven,
	And glose hem nouȝt for her good · to greven her soules! 367
Where do they deal with *poor* men, that have nothing to give them?	Y pray þe, where ben þei pryue · wiþ any pore wiȝtes,
	þat maie not amenden her hous · ne amenden hem-seluen?
	þei prechen in proude harte · & preiseþ her order,
	And werdliche worchype · wilneþ in erþe.
	Leeue it well, lef man · & men ryȝt-lokede, 372
They are prouder than Lucifer.	þer is more pryue pride · in prechours hertes
	þan þer lefte in Lucyfer · er he were lowe fallen;
	þey ben digne as dich water · þat dogges in bayteþ.
	Loke a ribaut of hem · þat can nouȝt wel reden 376
One who cannot say his Responds expounds the lawes.	His rewle ne his respondes · but be pure rote,
	Als as he were a connynge Clerke · he casteþ þe lawes,

355. *as digne*] so digne C.
356. *þei*] the BC. (Obs. the = they *frequently in* B.)
358. *medleth*] meddeley B (*cf. l.* 107); medeleth C.
359. *leeuen*] lyven B.
360. *biggeþ*] beggen (*over erasure*) B.
362. *Herdforþe*] Hartffourde B.
363. *leeue*] bcleve (*over erasure*) B.
364. [*ben* C] beyn A; bene B.
365. [*curry*] *Such is the reading; in* A *miswritten* carry; currey B; curreth C.
366. *lene hem*] leve hym B; leue hem C.
372. *Leeue*] Ken B (*but leave is written at end of l.* 371).
374. *er*] or C.
378. *casteþ*] *The* MS. *seems to have* hasteth, *perhaps for* kasteþ; kasteth B; casteth C.

Nouȝt lowli but lordly · & leesinges lyeþ.
For ryȝt as Menoures · most ypocricie vseþ,   380   Minorites are hypocrites, and Preachers proud.
Ryȝt so ben Prechers proude · purlyche in herte.
But, Cristen creatour · we Karmes first comen
Even in Elyes tyme · first of hem all,   But we Carmelites date from the
And lyven by our Lady · & lelly hir seruen   384   days of Elijah,
In clene comun life · kepen vs out of synne ;
Nowt proude as prechours beþ · but prayen full still   and pray for all that help us.
For all þe soules and þe lyves · þat we by lybbeth.
We connen on no queyntyse · (Crist wot þe soþe !) 388
But bysieþ vs in oure bedes · as vs best holdeþ.
And þerfore, leue leel man · leeue þat ich sygge,
A masse of vs mene men · is of more mede   Our masses are of most worth.
And passeth all praiers · of þies proude freers. 392
And þou wilt ȝyuen vs any good · y would þe here   Give us something, and you are pardoned;
    graunten
To taken all þy penance · in peril of my soule ;
And þouȝ þou conne nouȝt þy crede · clene þe assoile,   and never mind your Creed."
So þat þou mowe amenden our hous · wiþ money oþer
    elles,   396
Wiþ som katell oþer corne · or cuppes of siluer."
"TREWELY, frere," quaþ y þo · "to tellen þe þe soþe,   "I haven't a penny," said I;
    þer is no peny in my palke · to payen for my   "but teach me my Creed, and I will
    mete ;   do what I can."
I haue no good ne no gold · but go þus abouten,   400
And travaile full trewlye · to wynnen withe my fode.
But woldest þou for godes loue · lerne me my Crede,
Y schuld don for þy will · whan I wele hadde."
"Trewlie," quaþ þe frere · "a fol y þe holde !   404   "You must be a fool," said he,
þou woldest not weten þy fote · & woldest fich kacchen ! "like the cat that won't wet her feet."
Our pardon & oure preiers · so beþ þey nouȝt parted,

380. *Menoures*] mynors B   Min-   395. *conne nouȝt*] cannot B.
oures C.   396. *more*] now B.
388. *connen*] cannon B;   couuen   399. *palke*] palk B ; pakke C.
*C.   *on*] *struck through in B.   *soþe*]   403. *þy will*] the will B; the wil
southe C.   C.
393. *would*] woll B.   *þr*] ye *C. 406. *parted*] parten *C.
394. *in*] on B.

THE AUTHOR MEETS THE POOR PLOUGHMAN.

<small>I must go now to a housewife who has promised us ten pounds in her will.</small>

<small>I hope to get an Annuell for myself.</small>

<small>THE PLOUGH-MAN.</small>

<small>[¹ MS. "&"] Wandering on, I saw a ploughman, with a coarse coat, torn hood, and knobbed shoes.</small>

<small>He was in mud almost up to the ancle.</small>

Oure power lastiþ nouȝt so feer · but we some peny
fongen.
Fare well," quaþ þe frere · " for y mot heþen fonden,
And hyen to an houswife · þat haþ vs bequeþen.   409
Ten pounde in hir testament · to tellen þe soþe.
Ho draweþ to þe deþe-warde · but ȝet I am in drede
Lest ho turne her testament · & þerfore I hyȝe   412
To hauen hir to our hous · and henten ȝif y miȝte
An Anuell for myn owen [vse] · to helpen to cloþe."
" Godys forbode," quaþ [his] fellawe · " but ho forþ passe
Wil ho is in purpose · wiþ vs to departen ;   416
God let her no lenger lyven · for letteres ben manye."

Þanne turned y me forþe · and talked to my-selue
    Of þe falshede of þis folk · whou feiþles they
        [weren].
And as y wente be þe waie · wepynge for sorowe,   420
[I]¹ seiȝ a sely man me by · opon þe plow hongen.
His cote was of a cloute · þat cary was y-called,
His hod was full of holes · & his heer oute,
Wiþ his knopped schon · clouted full þykke ;   424
His ton toteden out · as he þe londe treddede,
His hosen ouerhongen his hokschynes · on eueriche a
        side,
Al beslombred in fen · as he þe plow folwede ;
Twey myteynes, as mete · maad all of cloutes ;   428
Þe fyngers weren for-werd · & ful of fen honged.
Þis whit waselede in þe [fen] · almost to þe ancle,
Foure roþeren hym by-forn · þat feble were [worþen] ;

<small>407. so feer] soffer B.
414. [vse BC] vs A.
415. [his BC] this A.
417. letteres] lettes ther (over erasure, and with ther above the line) B.
419. whou] how B; whow C. [weren C] werne A; werren B.
421. [I] I propose this reading; A has &; BC And.
426. hokschynes] hockshynes B (where ck is written over an erased k); hokshynes C. a] nearly erased in B.
427. beslombred] beslomered C.
428. mete] nettes (over erasure) B; meter *C.
429. forwerd] Forweryd B.
430. [fen B] fern A; feen C.
431. [worþen] Such should be the reading ; we find worþi A ; worthe B; worthi C; no doubt the original had worþē = worþen.</small>

Men myȝte reken ich a ryb · so reufull þey weren. 432
His wijf walked him wiþ · wiþ a longe gode, *His wife was beside him, in a*
In a cutted cote · cutted full heyȝe, *coat cut very short.*
Wrapped in a wynwe schete · to weren hire fro weders,
Barfote on þe bare ijs · þat þe blod folwede. 436
And at þe londes ende laye · a litell crom-bolle, *Their youngest child lay in a*
And þeron lay a litell childe · lapped in cloutes, *bowl, and two other children*
And tweyne of tweie ȝeres olde · opon a-noþer syde, *were beside them.*
And alle þey songen o songe · þat sorwe was to heren;
þey crieden alle o cry · a carefull note. 441
Þe sely man siȝede sore, & seide · "children, beþ stille!"
Þis man loked opon me · & leet þe plow stonden, *He asked me why I sighed so sore.*
And seyde, "sely man, why syȝest þou so harde? 444
Ȝif þe lakke lijflode · lene þe ich will
Swich good as God haþ sent · go we, leue broþer."
Y saide þanne, "naye, sire · my sorwe is wel more;
For y can nouȝt my Crede · y kare well harde; 448 *I told him, because I could*
For y can fynden no man · þat fully byleueþ, *not learn my Creed,*
To techen me þe heyȝe weie · & þerfore I wepe.
For y haue [fonded] þe freers · of þe foure orders, 451
For þere I wende haue wist · but now my wit lakkeþ;
And all my hope was on hem · & myn herte also; *though I had hoped the friars*
But þei ben fully feiþles · and þe fend sueþ." *would teach me.*
"A! broþer," quaþ he þo · "beware of þo foles! *"Beware of them," said he,*
For Crist seyde him-selfe · 'of swiche y ȝou warne,' 456 *"as Christ bade*
And false profetes in þe feiþ · he fulliche hem calde, *(Mat. vii. 15).*
'In vestimentis ouium · but onlie wiþ-inne
þei ben wilde wer-wolues · þat wiln þe folk robben.'
Þe fend founded hem first · þe feiþ to destroie, 460 *The fiend founded them.*

432. *reufull*] rewfulle B; rentful *C.
435. *wynwe*] wynow B.
437. *laye*] lath *C. *bolle*] bole B.
439. *olde*] elde B.
445. ȝif þe] yif thou B; Gif the C.
447. *wel*] myche B.
451. [*fonded*] *Such is the true reading; yet* ABC *have* fondes, *shewing a mistake in their common original. So also in l.* 6.
457. *hem*] hym B.
460. *fend*] fen *C.

And by his craft þei comen in · to combren þe chirche,
By þe couciteise of his craft · þe curates to helpen ;
But now þey hauen an hold · þey harmen full many.

They follow not their founders' rules.
Þei don nouȝt after Domynick · but drecheþ þe puple,
Ne folwen nouȝt Fraunces · but falslyche lybben, 465
And Austynes rewle · þei rekneþ but a fable,
But purchaseþ hem pryuylege · of popes at Rome.

They covet confessions and burials."
Þei coueten confessions · to kachen some hire,
And sepultures also · some wayten to cacchen ; 469
But oþer cures of Cristen · þei coueten nouȝt to haue,
But þere as wynnynge liþ · he lokeþ none oþer."

"What is your name ?" said I. He replied, "Piers the Ploughman."
"Whouȝ schal y nemne þy name · þat neiȝboures þe kalleþ ?" 472
"Peres," quaþ he, "þe pore man · þe plowe-man y hatte."

"A! Peres," quaþ y þo · "y pray þe, þou me telle

I asked him to tell me more of them,
More of þise tryflers · hou trechurly þei libbeþ ?
For ichon of hem haþ told me · a tale of þat oþer, 476
Of her wicked lijf · in werlde þat hy lybbeþ.

I trowe þat some wikked wyȝt · wrouȝte þis orders

and whether their rise was due to "Golias" or to Satan.
[þoruȝ] þat gleym of þat gest · þat Golias is y-calde,
Oþer ells Satan him-self · sente hem fro hell 480
To cumbren men wiþ her craft · Cristendome to schenden ?"

He replied that it was Satan's doing.
"Dere broþer," quaþ Peres · " þe devell is ful queynte ;
To encombren holy Chirche · he casteþ ful harde,

CAIM.
And furicheþ his falsnes · opon fele wise, 484
And fer he casteþ to-forn · þe folke to destroye.

"They are Cain's kindred, and like the Pharisees.
Of þe kynrede of Caym · he caste þe freres,
And founded hem on Farysens · feyned for gode ;

465. *Ne*] He *C.
468. *coueten*] So in C ; couetun A ; coveyton B. See l. 470.
469. *sepultures*] So in AB ; sepulturus *C. *cacchen*] kachen B ; lacchen C.
473. *hatte*] hott B.
476. *þat*] B omits.
477. *hy*] he BC.

479. [þoruȝ] *This excellent reading is suggested by* MS. B ; *which has* Thoughe, *altered to* Thorughe ; *we find* Trowe ye A ; Trow ye C ; *both are corruptions, due to the line above.*
484. *fele*] sely B.
486. *kynrede*] kyndred B.
487. *on*] or B. *Farysens*] Sarysenes *C. *gode*] good B ; God *C.

But þei wiþ her fals faiþ · michel folk schendeþ, 488
Crist calde hem him-self · kynde ypocrites ;
How often he cursed hem¹ · well can y tellen   [¹ MS. "heme."]
He seide ones him-self · to þat sory puple,   Christ called such men hypocrites
'Wo worþe ȝou, wyȝtes · wel lerned of þe lawe !' 492   (Luke xi. 46, 47).
Eft he seyde to hem-selfe · 'wo mote ȝou worþen,
þat þe toumbes of profetes · tildeþ vp heiȝe !
Ȝoure faderes fordeden hem · & to þe deþ hem brouȝte.'
Here y touche þis two · twynnen hem I þenke ; 496   Friars are just like Pharisees;
Who wilneþ ben wisere of lawe · þan lewde freres,   they like to be called *masters*,
And in multitude of men · ben maysters y-called,
And wilneþ worchips of þe werlde · & sitten wiþ heye,
And leueþ louynge of God · and lownesse behinde? 500
And in beldinge of tombes · þei trauaileþ grete   they build fine tombs.
To chargen her chirche-flore · and chaungen it ofte.
And þe fader of þe freers · defouled hir soules,   The father of friars is the devil.
þat was þe dygginge devel · þat drecheþ men ofte. 504
þe divill by his dotage · dissaueþ þe chirche,
And put in þe prechours · y-paynted wiþouten :   It was he who brought in the Preachers.
And by his queyntise þey comen in · þe curates to
  helpen,
But þat harmede hem harde · and halp hem full litell !
But Austines ordynaunce · was on a good trewþe, 509   Yet Austyn, Dominick, and
And also Domynikes dedes · weren [deruelich] y-vsed,   Francis founded them in truth.
And Frauncis founded his folke · fulliche on trewþe,
Pure parfit prestes · in penaunce to lybben,   512
In loue and in lownesse · & lettinge of pride,
Grounded on þe godspell · as God bad him-selue.
But now þe glose is so greit · in gladding tales   But now the

491. *ones*] ons BC.
493. *hemselfe*] hym-self B. ȝov] ye B.
494. *tildeþ*] tildith (*altered to* bildith) B; tildeth C.
496. *þis two*] theise tow B. *twynnen*] and twynnen B.
498. *in*] in a B.
499. *&*] and to B. *wiþ heye*] highe (*over erasure*) D.

501. *beldinge*] bulding B ; beldyng C; *but the true reading is probably* teldinge ; cf. ll. 181, 494.
503. *defouled*] desouled *C.
504. *dygginge*] digging B; dyggyng C.
507. *þe*] B *omits*.
510. [*deruelich*] derulich (*or* dernlich) A ; deruelich (*or* dernelich) B ; dernclich *C. *See* note.

2 *

Gospel is overlaid with glosses.	þat turneþ vp two-folde · vnteyned opon trewþe,	516
	þat þei bene cursed of Crist · y can hem well proue;	
	Wiþ-outen his blissinge · bare beþ þey in her werkes.	
Christ said, Blessed are the poor in spirit (Mat. v. 3).	For Crist seyde him-selfe · to swiche as him folwede,	
	'Y-blessed mote þei ben · þat mene ben in soule;'	520
	And alle pouere in gost · God him-self blisseþ.	
How many friars are thus poor? Try them, and see how touchy they are.	Whou fele freers fareþ so · fayn wolde y knowe!	
	Proue hem in proces · & pynch at her ordre,	
	And deme hem after þat þey don · & dredles, y leue	
	þei willn wexen pure wroþ · wonderliche sone,	525
	And schewen þe a scharp will · in a schort tyme,	
	To wilne wilfully wrapþe · & werche þerafter.	
WICLEFFE. Remember how they persecuted Wycliffe.	Wytnesse on Wycliff · þat warned hem wiþ trewþe;	
	For he in goodnesse of gost · graypliche hem warned	
	To waynen her wik[e]dnesse · & werkes of synne.	
	Whou sone þis sori men · [seweden] his soule,	
	And oueral lollede him · wiþ heretykes werkes!	532
	And so of þe blessinge of God · þei bereþ litel mede.	
Christ said, Blessed are the meek.	Afterward anoþer · onliche he blissede,	
	þe meke of þe [myddel-erde] · þouruȝ myȝt of his fader.	
	Fynd foure freres in a flok · þat folweþ þat rewle,	536
	þanne haue y tynt all my tast · touche and assaie!	
Blame friars a little, and, if they do not call thee 'liar'—	Lakke hem a litil wiȝt · & here lijf blame,	
	But he lepe vp on heiȝ · in hardynesse of herte,	
	And nemne þe anon nouȝt · & þi name lakke	540
	Wiþ proude wordes apert · þat passeth his rule,	
	Boþe wiþ ' þou leyest, & þou lext ' · in heynesse of sowle,	

517. *þei bene*] many bene B; they ben C.
521. *pouere*] power C.
522. *Whou*] how B.
525. *wexen*] A apparently has wexon, *with* x *and* o *imperfectly formed;* woxon B; wexon C; wexen *is better spelling.* *wroþ*] worthe B.
527. *wrapþe*] wrath B; wrathe C; *in* A *written so as to resemble* wrappe.
531. [*seweden*] *So in* BC; lewden A (*by mistake of* l *for* ſ).
535. [*myddel-erde*] *So in* C; myddel hertes A; myddell herth B (*which probably shews the spelling of the original*).
536. *þat rewle*] the rewle B.
539. *hardynesse*] herdnes B; hardenesse C.
540. *nemne*] *miswritten* memne A; nemne BC.
541. *apert*] apart B (*with the second* a *written over an erasure*).
542. *leyest — lext*] lyest and the lixst B; leyst and thou lext C.

And turne as a tyrant · þat turmenteþ him-selue,
A lord were loþere · for to leyne a k[n]aue 544 *why then*—a lord is *more reluctant* to give to a beggar than to them!
þanne swich a beggere · þe beste in a toun!
Loke nowe, leue man · beþ nouȝt þise i-lyke
Fully to þe Farisens · in fele of þise poyntes?
Al her brod beldyng · ben belded withe synne, 548
And in worchipe of þe werlde · her wynnynge þei
  holden;
þei schapen her chapolories · & streccheþ hem brode, Then they stretch out their scapulars, and spread on high their hems.
And launceþ heiȝe her hemmes · wiþ babelyng in stretes;
þei ben y-sewed wiþ whiȝt silk · & semes full queynte,
Y-stongen wiþ stiches · þat stareþ as siluer. 553
And but freres ben first y-set · at sopers & at festes, They must be set first at feasts,
þei wiln ben wonderly wroþ · ywis, as y trowe;
But þey ben at þe lordes borde · louren þey willeþ,
He mot bygynne þat borde · a beggere, (wiþ sorwe!)
And first sitten in se · in her synagoges, 558 and receive honour in their minsters.
þat beþ here heyȝe helle-hous · of Kaymes kynde!
For þouȝ a man in her mynster · a masse wolde heren,
His siȝt schal so [be] set · on sundrye werkes,
þe penounes & þe pomels · & poyntes of scheldes The arms and peunons there destroy devotion.
Wiþ-drawen his deuocion · & dusken his herte;
I likne it to a lym-ȝerde · to drawen men to hell, 564
And to worchipe of þe fend · to wrappen þe soules.
And also Crist him-selfe seide · to swiche ypocrites, Christ said, They love greetings in the markets (Mat. xxiii. 7),
'He loueþ in markettes ben met · wiþ gretynges of
  pouere,
And lowynge of lewed men · in Lent[e]nes tyme.' 568
For þei han of bichopes y-bouȝt · wiþ her propre siluer,

543. *turne*] turnnen C.
544. *loþer*] lether B. *leyne*] beyne B (*with* b *over erasure*). knaue BC.
546. *beþ*] beth BC: *in* A *apparently written* beþ.
548. *belding*] bilding B. *belded*] bylded B.
550. *schapen*] sharpen B. *chapolories*] capolories B. *brode*] abrode B.
551. *launceþ*] launceth C.
552. *&*] B *omits*.
557. *þat*] the B.
559. *helle-hous*] helle houndes (!) B.
561. [*be*] *So in* B; *by* AC.
562. *penounes*] penonnes C.
568. *Lentenes* C] Lentues A; Lentonys B.

THEY PERVERT THE SCRIPTURES.

  And purchased of penaunce · þe puple to assoile.
  But money may maken · mesur of þe peyne,
  (After þat his power is to payen) · his penance schal
   faile;   572
  (God leue it be a good help · for hele of þe soules!)

and to be called of men, Rabbi, Rabbi; And also þis myster men · ben maysters icalled,
  þat þe gentill Iesus · generallyche blamed,
  And þat poynt to his apostells · purly defended. 576

But friars have forgotten whether or not their founders wished them to become masters. But freres hauen forȝetten þis · (and þe fend suweþ,
  He þat maystri louede · Lucifer þe olde),
  Wher Fraunceis or Domynik · oþer Austen ordeynide
  Any of þis dotardes · doctur to worþe,   580
  Masters of dyvinitie · her matens to leue,
  And chereliche as a cheueteyne · his chambre to holden
  Wiþ chymene & chapell · & chesen whan him liste,
  And serued as a souereine · & as a lorde sitten. 584

Such a man overlays God's words with glosses. Swiche a gome godes wordes · grysliche gloseþ ;
  Y trowe, he toucheþ nouȝt þe text · but takeþ it for a
   tale.

Christ said, Do not ye premeditate (Mark xiii. 11). God forbad to his folke · & fullyche defended 587
  þey schulden nouȝt stodyen biforn · ne sturen her wittes,
  But sodenlie þe [same] word · with her mowþ schewe
  þat weren ȝeuen hem of God · þoruȝ gost of him-selue.

But friars meditate over their legends. Now mot a frere studyen · & stumblen in tales,
  And leuen his matynes · & no masse singen,   592
  And loken hem lesynges · þat likeþ þe puple,
  To purchasen him his pursfull · to paye for þe drynke.

After harvest come the friars, And broþer, when bernes ben full · & holly tyme passed,

---

572. *After þat*] For as B (*over an erasure*). *payen*] peye so B (*with so over erasure*).
 573. *lene*] leve B ; leue C.
 574. *myster*] mynster B.
 575. *gentill*] genltil (*sic*) C.
 577. *suweþ*] The original must have had *fuweþ* ; A *has* fu luweth, *with* fu *struck through* ; sewith B ; suweth C.
 579. *Wher*] Nor (*over erasure*) B;

Where C.
 580. *doctur—worþe*] B *has* doctur to worth, *which is struck out, and followed by* pryde for to suen ; *where* suen *is afterwards altered to* ensewen.
 583. *chesen*] chosen C.
 589. [*same*] *So in* BC; A *has* some.
 590. *himseluc*] hem selue C.
 595. *bernes*] barnys B. *holly*] *So in* AB ; holy C.

þanne comen cursed freres · & croucheþ full lowe ; 596   *and beg something at every house.*
A losel, a lymitour · ouer all þe lond lepeþ,
And loke, þat he leue non house · þat somwhat he ne lacche ;
And þer þei gilen hem-self · & godes worde turneþ.
Bagges and beggyng · he bad his folk leuen,   600   *Christ said, Take no thought for your life (Mat. vi. 25).*
And only seruen him-self · & hijs rewle sechen,
And all þat nedly nedeþ · þat schuld hem nouȝt lakken.
Whereto beggen þise men · and ben nouȝt so feble ;   *Why do these men beg, not being maimed or in lack of meat ?*
(Hem faileþ no furrynge · ne cloþes at full),   604
But for a lustfull lijf · in lustes to dwellen ?
Wiþ-outen any trauaile · vntrewliche [hy] lybbeth.
Hy beþ nouȝt maymed men · ne no mete lakkeþ,
Y-cloþed in curious cloþ · & clenliche arayed.   608
It is a laweles lijf · as lordynges vsen,   *They live like lords.*
Neyþer ordeyned in ordir · but onlie libbeþ.
Crist bad blissen · bodies on erþe   611   *Christ said, Blessed are ye*
þat wepen for wykkednes · þat he byforne wrouȝte ;— *that weep now (Luke vi. 21).*
þat ben fewe of þo freres · for þei ben ner dede *But friars never weep till they are*
And put all in pur [claþ] · wiþ pottes on her hedes ; *all but dead ;*
þanne [he] waryeþ & wepeþ · & wicheþ after heuen,
And fyeþ on her falshedes · þat þei bifore deden ;   616
And þerfore of þat blissinge · trewlie, as y trowe,   *small blessing will be theirs*
þei may trussen her part · in a terre powȝe !
All þo blissed beþ · þat bodyliche hungreþ ;— *Christ said, Blessed are ye*
þat ben þe pore penyles · þat han ouer-passed   620 *that hunger now, meaning such as*
þe poynt of her pris lijf · in penaunce of werkes, *are past work,*

---

596. *comen*] In A *loosely written, resembling* cornen ; comen BC.
598. *he*] ye B.   *lacche*] latche C.
600. *Bagges*] to bagges B (*to written in the margin*).   *leuen*] lyven B.
601. *hijs*] *So in* AB, *and no doubt in their original;* C *has the simpler form* his.
604. *at*] atte C.
606. [*hy*] *Inserted to shew the sense more clearly; not in* ABC.

608. *Y-cloþed*] Thei clothed *C. *cloþ*] clothes B.
610. *onlie*] oneth B ; onethe C.
614. [*claþ*] *Suggested by* C, *which has* clath ; *in* A *it is written* clay ; B *has* cleye ; *see note.*
615. [*he* BC] ho A.   *wicheþ*] whissbith B.
618. *trussen*] trullen B (*by mistaking* f *for* l). *terre powȝe*] tree ploughe (*altered to* poghe) B ; terre powghe C.
621. *of* (2)] and B.

THEY ARE CRUEL AND REVENGEFUL.

    And mown nouʒt swynken ne sweten · but ben swyþe feble,
or maimed, or lepers. Oþer maymed at myschef · or meseles syke,
    And here good is a-gon · & greueþ hem to beggen. 624
    þer is no frer in feiþ · þat fareþ in þis wise;
But unless a friar can beg well, he is soon made away with. But he maie beggen his bred · his bed is ygreiþed;
    Vnder a pot he schal be put · in a pryvie chambre,
    þat he schal lyuen ne last · but litell while after! 628
Blessed are the merciful; Al-miʒti god & man · þe merciable blessed
    þat han mercy on men · þat misdon hem here;—
    But whoso for-gabbed a frere · y-founden at þe stues,
    And brouʒte blod of his bodi · on bak or on side, 632
but one had better harm a lord than a friar. Hym were as god greuen · a greit lorde of rentes.
    He schulde sonner bene schryven · (schortlie to tellen)
    þouʒ he kilde a comlye knyʒt · & compased his morþer,
    þanne a buffet to beden · a beggere frere. 636
Blessed are the pure in heart; þe clene hertes Crist · he curtey[s]liche blissed,
    þat [coueten] no katel · but Cristes full blisse,
    þat leeueþ fulliche on God · & lellyche þenkeþ
    On his lore and his lawe · & lyueþ opon trewþe;— 640
but friars follow another rule. Freres han forʒeten þis · & folweþ an oþer;
    þat þei may henten, þey holden · by-hirneþ it sone.
    Heir hertes ben clene y-hid · in her hiʒe cloistre,
    As kurres from kareyne · þat is cast in dyches! 644
Blessed are the peacemakers; but a friar's sting is worse than a wasp's. And parfite Crist · þe pesible blissed,
    þat bene suffrant & sobre · & susteyne anger;—
    A-say of her sobernesse · & þou miʒt y-knowen,
    þer is no waspe in þis werlde · þat will wilfullok[e]r styngen, 648

---

623. *maymed*] mayned *C. *syke*] lyke *C.
631. *for-gabbed*] So in BC; in A *resembles* forgalbed.
635. *morþer*] morther B; mother *C.
637. *Crist*] of crist AB; C *omits* of, *and it seems better to do so.* *curteysliche*] curteyliche ABC (*wrongly, because wrong in their common original*).
638. [*coueten* C] couetyne A; coveyten B. *blisse*] bles B.
643. *y-hid*] yhad B.
648. *wilfulloker*] wilfullokr A; wilfuller B; folloke *C. Cf. l. 527.

For stappyng on a too · of a styncande frere!
For neþer souereyn ne soget · þei ne suffreþ neuer;
All þe blissing of God · beouten þei walken;
For of her suffraunce, for soþe · men seþ but litell! 652
Alle þat persecution · in pure lijf suffren,   *Blessed are they which are perse-*
þei han þe benison of god · blissed in erþe;—   *cuted for right-*
Y praie, parceyue now · þe pursut of a frere,   *eousness' sake.*
In what measure of meknesse · þise men deleþ. 656
Byhold opon Wat Brut · whou bisiliche þei pursueden *Remember how they persecuted*
For he seyde hem þe soþe · & ʒet, syre, ferþore,   *Walter Brute,*
Hy may no more marren [hym] · but men telleþ
þat he is an heretike · and yuele byleueþ,   660
And prechiþ it in pulpit · to blenden þe puple; *and preached that he was a heretic.*
þei wolden awyrien þat wiʒt · for his well dedes;
And so þei chewen charitie · as chewen schaf houndes.
And þei pursueþ þe poucre · & passeþ pursutes, 664
Boþe þey wiln & þei wolden · y-worþen so grete
To passen any mans miʒt · to morþeren þe soules; *They would gladly murder a man's*
First to brenne þe bodye · in a bale of fijr, 667 *soul, having first burnt his body.*
And syþen þe sely soule slen · & senden hyre to helle!
And Crist clerlie forbadde · his Cristene, & defended *And Christ said, Judge not accord-*
þei schulden nouʒt after þe face · neuer þe folke *ing to the appear-*
   demen;"—   *ance"—*
"Sur," y seide my-self · "þou semest to blamen. *"Sir," said I, "why despise*
Why dispisest þou þus · þise sely pore freres, 672 *these poor friars?*
None oþer men so mychel · monkes ne preistes,
Chanons ne Charthous · þat in chirche serueth?
It semeþ þat þise sely men · han somwhat þe greued *Have they grieved you in any way?"*
Oþer wiþ word or wiþ werke · & þerfore þou wilnest

649. *stappyng*] stamping B. *styn-cande*] *resembles* styntande *in* A, *owing to confusion between* c *and* t; stynkande B; styncand C.
651. *þe*] thei C. *beouten*] bene outten B.
652. *seþ*] say B; sey C.
657. *Wat*] Water BC.
659. *Hy*] he B. [*hym*] *required*

by the sense; ABC *have* hem.
661. *in*] in the B.
663. *chewen*] shewin B. *chewen*] shewen B. *schaf*] shaffen B; shaf C.
669. *forbadde*] *loosely written as* forladde A; forbad BC.
671. *Sur*] But B; Sire C.
674. *charthous*] charter house B.

> To schenden oþer [schamen] hem · wiþ þi sharpe speche,
> And harmen holliche · & her hous greuen?"

"Nay," said he, "I speak for the good of thy soul.
> "I praie þe," quaþ Peres · " put þat out of þy mynde;
> Certen for sowle hele · y saie þe þis wordes. 680

The monks are not much better than the friars,
> Y preise nouȝt possessioners · but pur lytel;
> For falshed of freres · haþ fulliche encombred
> Manye of þis maner men · & maid hem to leuen

but have been led astray by them.
> Here charite & chastete · & [chesen] hem to lustes, 684
> And waxen to werldly · and wayuen þe trewþe,
> And leuen þe loue of her God · and þe werlde seruen.
> But for falshed of freres · y fele in my soule,
> (Seynge þe synfull lijf) · þat sorweþ myn herte 688

Friars are falsely clothed in white, like angels or elders.
> How þei ben cloþed in cloþ · þat clennest scheweþ;
> For aungells & Arcangells · all þei whijt vseþ,
> And alle Aldermen · þat bene *ante tronum.*
> þise tokens hauen freres taken · but y trowe þat a fewe
> Folwen fully þat cloþ · but falsliche þat vseþ. 693

White betokens cleanness in soul.
> For whijt in trowþe bytokneþ · clennes in soule;
> Ȝif he haue vnder-neþen whijt · þanne he aboue wereþ,

Black, sorrow for our sin.
> Blak, þat bytokneþ · bale for oure synne,
> And mournynge for misdede · of hem þat þis vseþ, 697
> And serwe for synfull lijf; · so þat cloþ askeþ.

Friars weep not for sin, but feed on it.
> Y trowe þer ben nouȝt ten freres · þat for synne wepen,
> For þat lijf is here lust · & þereyn þei libben 700
> In fraitour & in fermori · her fostringe is synne;
> It is her mete at iche a mel · her most sustenaunce.

Note how St Hildegarde says
> Herkne opon Hyldegare · hou homliche he telleþ
> How her sustenaunce is synne; · & syker, as y trowe,

---

677. *oþer*] or B. [*schamen*] shamen BC; A *here repeats* schenden. *þi*] the *C.
678. *harmen*] *So too in* B; hannen *C.
681. *possessioners*] pocessioners B; pocessioneres C.
684. [*chesen*] *miswritten as* schosen A; chosen B; shosen *C; *see* l. 583.
685. *werldly*] worldly B; werly C. *wayuen*] waynen *C.
691—693. *Written in margin in* B, *and* l. 693 *corruptly given.*
694. *in*] of B.
700. *þereyn*] therby BC. *þei*] thi*C.
703. *opon Hyldegare*] open Hildegare B; (*and over it is written of* Lidgate (!!) *as a gloss*).

Weren her confessiones · clenli destrued, 705 *their sustenance is sin.*
Hy schulde nouȝt beren hem so bragg · ne [belden] so heyȝe,
(For þe fallynge of synne · socoureþ þo foles);
And bigileþ þe grete · wiþ glauerynge wordes, 708 *They beguile the great with flattery.*
Wiþ glosinge of godspells · þei gods worde turneþ,
And pasen all þe pryuylege · þat Petur after vsed.
Þe power of þe Apostells · þei pasen in speche,
For to sellen þe synnes · for siluer oþer mede, 712 *They sell pardons for money,*
And purlyche *a pena* · þe puple assoileþ,
And *a culpa* also · þat þey may kachen
Money oþer money-worthe · & mede to fonge,
And bene at lone & at bode · as burgeses vsithe. 716
Þus þey seruen Satanas · & soules bygileþ, *and serve Satan.*
Marchantes of malisons · mansede wreches!
Þei vsen russet also · somme of þis freres, *Some of them wear russet,*
Þat bitokneþ trauaile · & trewþe opon erþe ;— 720 *which means hard labour.*
Bote loke whou þis lorels · labouren þe erþe,
But freten þe frute þat þe folk · full lellich biswynkeþ ;
Wiþ trauail of trewe men · þei tymbren her houses, *But they build their houses with the earnings of others.*
And of þe curious cloþe · her copes þei biggen ; 724
And [als] his getynge is greet · he schal ben good holden,
And ryȝt as dranes doþ nouȝt · but drynkeþ vp þe huny, *As drones drink the honey which bees have gathered,*
Whan been wiþe her bysynesse · han brouȝt it to hepe,
Riȝt so.fareþ freres · wiþ folke opon erþe ; 728
Þey freten vp þe fu[r]ste-froyt · & falsliche lybbeþ. *so friars eat up the first-fruits,*
But alle freres eten nouȝt · y-lich good mete,
But after þat his wynnynge is · is his well-fare ;
And after þat he bringeþ home · his bed schal ben grayþed ; 732 *each one according to what he has got by begging.*

705. *clenli*] cleerly (*over erasure*) B. abode (!) B.
706. [*belden*] *So in* BC; *in* A *mis-* 722. *freten*] Ferton B.
written helden. 725. [*als* BC] all A.
707. þo] the C. 728. *fareþ*] Farith the B.
716. *lone & at bode*] love & at 729. *freten*] Fretton B.

And after þat his rychesse is rauȝt · he schal ben redy
serued.
But see þi-self in þi siȝt · whou somme of hem walkeþ

Some go poorly clad, whilst his fellow wears red shoes,

Wiþ cloutede schon · & cloþes ful feble,
Wel neiȝ for-werd · & þe wlon offe ;   736
And his felawe in a froke · worþ swiche fiftene,
A-rayd in rede sc[h]on · (& elles were reuþe !)
And sexe copes or seven · in his celle hongeþ.
þouȝ for fayling of good · his fellawe schulde sterue, 740

and will not give him a penny.

He wolde nouȝt lenen him a peny · his lijf for to holden.
Y miȝt tymen þo troiflardes · to toilen wiþ þe erþe,
Tylyen & trewliche lyven · & her flech tempren !

[¹ MS. Nov.]

Now ¹ mot ich soutere his sone · setten to schole,   744

Now, every beggar's brat learns to write ;

And ich a beggers brol · on þe booke lerne,
And worþ to a writere · & wiþ a lorde dwell,
Oþer falsly to a frere · þe fend for to seruen !
So of þat beggers brol · a bychop schal worþen,   748
Among þe peres of þe lond · prese to sitten,

and lords' sons bow down to them.

And lordes sones lowly · to þo losells aloute,
Knyȝtes croukeþ hem to · & crucheþ full lowe ;
And his syre a soutere · y-suled in grees,   752
His teeþ wiþ toylinge of leþer · tatered as a sawe !

Alas! that lords believe them and give to them!

Alaas ! þat lordes of þe londe · leueþ swiche wrechen,
And leueþ swiche lorels · for her lowe wordes !
þey schulden maken bichopes · her owen breþren childre,

Bishops should be of gentle blood, not of such as these.

Oþer of some gentil blod · & so it best semed,   757
And foster none faytoures · ne swiche false freres
To maken fatt & full · & her fleche combren !

Their nature is better suited to cleaning ditches.

For her kynde were more · to y-clense diches   760
þan ben to sopers y-set first · and serued wiþ siluer !

---

736. *forwerd*] Forweryd B.   *wlon*] *and alliteration.*
So in AC ; wolne B.
738. *schon*] *See* l. 735 ; scon A ;
sone (*altered to* scone) B ; stone *C.
routhe] renthe *C.
739. *hongeþ*] hongid B.
740. *good*] *Perhaps we should read*
food, *for this improves both the sense*

744. *schole*] skale B.
745. *brol*] brawle B.
748. *brol*] brawle B.   *bychop*]
bushope B ; Abbot *C.
755. *leneth*] leueth C.
756. *bichopes*] Abbottes *C.

A great bolle-full of benen · were betere in his wombe, Beans and bacon would suit them better than partridges or plovers.
And wiþ þe randes of bakun · his baly for to fillen,
þan pertriches or plouers · or pekokes y-rosted, 764
And comeren her stomakes · wiþ curious drynkes,
þat makeþ swiche harlottes · hordome vsen,
And wiþ her wicked worde · wymmen bitraieþ!
God wold her wonynge · were in wildernesse, 768
And fals freres forboden · þe fayre ladis chaumbres! Would that they were forbidden the fair ladies' chambers
For knewe lordes her craft · trewlie, y trowe,
þey schulden nouȝt haunten her hous · so homly on niȝtes,
Ne bedden swiche broþels · in so brode schetes, 772
But scheten her heued in þe stre · to scharpen her wittes; Lords should not give them sheets, but shut their heads in the straw.
Ne ben kynges confessours of custom · ne þe counsell of þe rewme knowe!
For Fraunces founded hem nouȝt · to faren on þat wise,
Ne Domynik dued hem neuer · swiche drynkers to worþe, 776
Ne Helye ne Austen · swiche lijf neuer vsed, Their founders never lived as they do.
But in pouerte of spirit · spended her tyme.
We haue sene our-self · in a schort tyme,
Whou freres wolden no flech · among þe folke vsen; Once they would eat no flesh, but they have sunk that rule—for the love of our Lord
But now þe harlottes · han hid thilke rewle, 781
And, for þe loue of oure lorde · haue leyd hire in water.
Wenest þou þer wold so fele · swiche warlawes worþen,
Ne were wordlyche wele · & her welfare?
þei schulden deluen & diggen · & dongen þe erþe, They ought to dig and delve, and eat common bread, and vegetables without meat, and work and go roughly clad."
And mene mong-corn bred · to her mete fongen, 786
And wortes flechles wroughte · & water to drinken,
And werchen & wolward gon · as we wrecches vsen;

762. *benen*] beuen *C.
763. *randes*] bandes BC.
769. *þe*] B *omits*.
771. *homly*] hōly C.
773. *scheten*] shottin B; sheten C.
782. *oure*] the B.
783. *Wenest þou*] Wenestowe B.
785. *diggen*] dyken BC.
786. *menemong*] mene mogge B. *to*] and B.

An aunter ȝif þer wolde on · amonge an hol hundred
Lyuen so for godes loue · in tyme of a wynter!" 790

"But, Piers," said I, "teach me my Creed."
"Leue Peres," quaþ y þo · "y praie þat þou me tell
Whou y maie conne my Crede · in Cristen beleue?"
"Leue broþer," quaþ he · "hold þat y segge,
I will techen þe þe trewþe · & tellen þe þe soþe." 794

CREDO.

The Creede. Believe on God who made the world;
Leue þou on oure Louerd God · þat all þe werld
wrouȝte,
Holy heuen opon hey · hollyche he fourmede, 796
And is almiȝti him-self · ouer all his werkes,
And wrouȝt as his will was · þe we[r]lde and þe heuen;

and on Jesu Christ, his only Son, conceived of the Holy Ghost,
And on gentyl Jesu Crist · engendred of him-seluen,
His own onlyche sonne · Lord ouer all y-knowen, 800
[þat] was clenly conseued · clerlye, in trewþe,
Of þe hey Holy Gost · þis is þe holy beleue;

born of the maiden Mary,
And of þe mayden Marye · man was he born,
Wiþ-outen synnfull sede · þis is fully þe beleue; 804

crowned with thorn, crucified, dead, and buried;
Wiþ þorn y-crouned, crucified · & on þe crois dyede,
And syþen his blissed body · was in a ston byried,

who descended into hell, and fetched thence our forefathers, ascended into heaven, and sitteth on the Father's right hand,
And descended a-doune · to þe derk helle,
And fet oute our formfaderes · & hy full feyn weren;
Þe þridde daye rediliche · him-self ros fram deeþ, 809
And on a ston þere he stod · he steiȝ vp to heuene,
And on his fader riȝt hand · redeliche he sitteþ,
Þat al-miȝti god · ouer all oþer whyȝtes;

whence he shall come to judge the quick and the dead;
And is hereafter to komen · Crist, all him-seluen,
To demen þe quyke and þe dede · wiþ-outen any doute;

and in the Holy Ghost; the Catholic church;
And in þe heiȝe holly gost · holly y beleue, 815
And generall holy chirche also · hold þis in þy mynde;
[*The communion of sayntes · for soth I to the sayn;*

789. *An aunter*] A Vanter B; *In A*, An aunter ȝif *is miswritten* An aunterȝ if.
796. *opon*] eth on *C.
798. *werlde*] worlde B; werld C.
801. [*þat*] that BC; It A.

804. *þe*] thy B.
810. *steiȝ*] *miswritten* striȝ *in* A; stigh B; steigh C.
812. *whyȝtes*] whight ys B.
817—821. *In C only; see* note. *These lines are spurious.*

And for our great sinnes · forgiuenes for to getten, *[Fiue lines added in 1553.]*
And only by Christ · clenlich to be clensed ;
Our bodies again to risen · right as we been here, 820
And þe liif euerlasting · leue ich to habben ; Amen.]
And in þe [sacrement] also · þat soþfast God on is, *And in the*
(Fullich his fleche & his blod) · þat for vs deþe þolede.— *Presence in the sacrament,*
And þouȝ þis flaterynge freres · wyln for her pride, 824
Disputen of þis deyte · as dotardes schulden,
Þe more þe matere is moved · þe [masedere hy] worþen. *which friars dispute about;*
Lat þe losels alone · & leue þou¹ þe trewþe,
For Crist seyde it is so · so mot it nede worþe ; 828 *[¹ MS. you]*
Þerfore studye þou¹ nouȝt þeron · ne stere þi wittes,
It is his blissed body · so bad he vs beleuen. *which cannot be explained,*
  Þise maystres of dyvinitie · many, als y trowe,
Folwen nouȝt fully þe feiþ · as fele of þe lewede. 832
Whouȝ may mannes wijt · þoruȝ werk [of] him-selue,
Knowen Cristes pryuitie · þat all kynde passeþ ?
It mot ben a man · of also mek an herte, *It is meek-hearted*
Þat myȝte wiþ his good lijf · þat Holly Gost fongen ; *men that receive the Holy Ghost.*
And þanne nedeþ him nouȝt · neuer for to studyen ; 837
He miȝte no maistre [ben] kald · (for Crist þat defended),
Ne puten [no] pylion · on his pild pate ;
But prechen in parfite lijf · & no pride vsen. 840
  But all þat euer I haue seyd · soþ it me semeþ,
And all þat euer I haue writen · is soþ, as I trowe, *All that I have ever written is*
And for amending of þise men · is most þat I write : *true, as I suppose.*
God wold hy wolden ben war · & werchen þe better !
  But, for y am a lewed man · paraunter y miȝte *I speak not with*
Passen par auenture · & in som poynt erren, 846 *authority, but ask*

822, 823. *Not in* C; *see note.*
822. [*sacrement* B] sacremens A.
825. þis] Godes C. deyte] diet B.
826. *masedere hy*] *So in* C; masedere hi B ; A *corruptly has* mose dere by.
828—830. *Not in* C.
831. þise] theise B ; For these C.
833 [*of* BC] *or* A. *wijt*] wit B.

836. þat *Holly*] the holly B ; the holy C.
838. [*ben* C] bene B ; *in* A *miswritten* þen.
839. [*no* BC] on A.
845. *paraunter*] paraventure B.
846. *par auenture*] paraventur B ; par aduenture C.

pardon if I have missaid.

Y will nouȝt þis matere · maistrely auowen ;
But ȝif ich haue myssaid · mercy ich aske,   848
& praie all maner men · þis matere amende,
Iche a word by him-self · & all, ȝif it nedeþ.

God save all faithful friars, and amend all that are false!

God of his grete myȝte · & his good grace
Saue all freres · þat faiþfully lybben,   852
And alle þo þat ben fals · fayre hem amende,
And ȝyue hem wijt & good will · swiche dedes to werche
þat þei maie wynnen þe lif · þat euer schal lesten !
AMEN.   855

854. *wijt*] wyt B ; wiit C.

NOTES.

LINE 1. *Cros*, the cross. Alluding probably to the mark of a cross which was sometimes prefixed to the *beginning* of a piece of writing, especially of an alphabet in a primer. See *Notes and Queries*, 3rd S. xi. 352. The alliteration in this line is defective, and it scans badly.

6. *patred*. The readings are, patres, AC; partes B; but neither of these make sense, whilst the following extract shews that *patred* is the right word.

"Ever he *patred* on theyr names faste,
That he had them in ordre at the laste."
How the Plowman lerned his Paternoster:
Hazlitt's Early Pop. Poetry, vol. i. p. 215.

17. And if = an if, i. e. if. The spelling *and* for *an* is not uncommon; it still stands, e. g., in our Bibles, Mat. xxiv. 48, and *and* = *if* in Lancelot of the Laik, l. 1024.

couþe, teach; *sub.* the Creed.

20. *wilneþ*, desireth: the writer distinguishes between *wille* and *wilncþ*; cf. l. 17.

25. *leueden*, believed; *leuen* (believe) would suit the context better.

27. *for-þan*, A.S. *for-þan, for-þam*, from *for* and *þam* (dat. case of the demonstrative pronoun *se, seò, þæt*); for that, with a view to that. The sense is, "But, by questioning them with a view to finding out what they know, many are there found to fail."

28. This interview with the Minorite was doubtless suggested by Passus IX of Piers Plowman (Text A). There, William asks two Minorites if they know where Do-wel is, whereupon—"Mari, (quod þe Menour) · Among vs he dweleþ," &c. See the Preface.

29. *foure ordres*. See Massingberd; Hist. of Reformation, chap. vii., on "The Mendicant Orders; their rise and history." A few of the most useful facts about the four orders of friars are here collected for convenience, arranged in the order in which they are more fully spoken of further on. They were,

(1.) The Minorites, Franciscans, or *Gray* Friars, called in France *Cordeliers*. Called Franciscans, from their founder, St Francis of Assisi;

Minorites (in Italian, *Frati Minori*, in French, *Frères Mineurs*), as being, as he said, the humblest of the religious foundations; Gray Friars, from the colour of their habit; and *Cordeliers*, from the hempen cord with which they were girded. For further details, see *Monumenta Franciscana*, which tells us that they were fond of physical studies, made much use of Aristotle, preached pithy sermons, exalted the Virgin, encouraged marriages, and were the most popular of the orders, but at last degenerated into a compound of the pedlar or huckster with the mountebank or quack doctor. See Mrs Jameson's Legends of the Monastic orders, and the Life of St Francis in Sir J. Stephen's Ecclesiastical Biography. They arrived in England in A.D. 1224. Friar Bacon was a Franciscan.

(2.) The Dominicans, Black Friars, Friars Preachers, or Jacobins. Founded by St Dominick, of Castile; order confirmed by Pope Honorius in A.D. 1216; arrived in England about 1221. Habit, a white woollen gown, with white girdle; over this, a white scapular; over these, a *black* cloak with a hood, whence their name. They were noted for their fondness for preaching, their great knowledge of scholastic theology, their excessive pride, and the splendour of their buildings. The Black *Monks* were the Benedictines.

(3.) The Augustine or Austin Friars, so named from St Augustine of Hippo. They clothed in black, with a leathern girdle. They were first congregated *into one body* by Pope Alexander IV., under one Lanfranc, in 1256. They are distinct from the Augustine *Canons*.

(4.) The Carmelites, or *White* Friars, whose dress was white, over a dark-brown tunic. They pretended that their order was of the highest antiquity and derived from Helias, i. e. the prophet Elijah; that a succession of anchorites had lived in Mount Carmel from his time till the thirteenth century; and that the Virgin was the special protectress of their order. Hence they were sometimes called "Maries men," as at l. 48, with which cf. l. 384.

As the *priority* of the foundation of the orders is so often discussed in the poem, I add that the dates of their *first* institution are, Augustines, 1150; Carmelites, 1160; Dominicans, 1206; Franciscans, 1209.

31. MS. A. is here obviously corrupt.

32. The reading *wittede* is a mistake made from confusion with *wyten*. *Wende* (I weened) is the true past tense of *wenen*; as in l. 452.

41. *that thou madde*, that thou art mad. Mr Wright printed "that thou [art] madde;" but cf. l. 280, and Chau. Mil. Ta., l. 373.

43. *jugulers.* See Tyrwhitt's Chaucer; note to Cant. Tales, v. 11453. The *jougleurs* or *jogelors* (*joculatores*) were originally minstrels who could perform feats of sleight of hand, &c., but they soon became mere mountebanks, and the name became, as here, a term of contempt. We read of "*jogulors*, dremers, and rafars," (*reavers, spoilers*); see Apology attributed to Wycliffe; (Camden Soc.) p. 96.

43. *iapers, of kynde*, jesters, by nature. Cf.

"Bote *Iapers* and Iangelers · Iudas Children."
Piers Plowman, A. *prol.* 35 (ed. Skeat, 1867).

44. *Lorels* and *losels* (used further on) are much the same word. We find in the Glosse of Spenser's Shepheard's Calendar (August) the following: "*Lorrell*, a losell;" which shews that the latter form was the one longest used.

46. *gestes*, legends, tales; see Tyrwhitt's Chaucer; note to v. 13775.

48. Compare,

"Horum quidam prædicant quod sunt ex *Maria*;
Alii tamen asserunt quod sunt ex Helia."—*Pol. Poems*, i. 262.

"The Carmelites, sometimes called the brethren of the blessed Virgin, were fond of boasting their familiar intercourse with the Virgin Mary. Among other things, they pretended that the Virgin assumed the Carmelite habit and profession; and that she appeared to Simon Sturckius, general of their order, in the thirteenth century, and gave him a solemn promise, that the souls of those Christians who died with the Carmelite scapulary upon their shoulders, should infallibly escape damnation."—*Warton, Hist. Eng. Poet.* ii. 132; ed. 1824.

Hone (Ancient Mysteries, p. 281) reminds us that some of the most absurd tales told by the Carmelites have been not very long ago revived in "A Short Treatise of the Antiquity, Privileges, &c., of the Confraternity of our Blessed Lady of Mount Carmel." (London, 1796, 18mo.)

54. *to fynde*; compare the phrase, to *find* one in meat and drink.

65. *freres of the Pye*. These were the Fratres de Pica (Walsingham, Hist. Anglicana, i. 182); they were called *Pied Friars* from their dress being a mixture of black and white, like a magpie.

"With an O and an I, fuerunt *Pyed Freres*,
Quomodo mutati sunt, rogo dicat Pers."
Pol. Poems, i. 262.

67. *glut* = A.S. *gluto*, a glutton.

70. "People may bequest their money, &c." A line seems lost between 69 and 70.

72. "*Robartes men*, or Roberdsmen, were a set of lawless vagabonds, notorious for their outrages when Pierce Plowman was written. The statute of Edward the Third (an. reg. 5, c. xiv) specifies 'divers manslaughters, felonies, and robberies, done by people that be called *Roberdesmen*, Wastours, and drawlatches.' And the statute of Richard the Second (an. reg. 7, c. v.) ordains, that the statute of King Edward concerning *Roberdsmen* and *Drawlacches* shall be rigorously observed. Sir Edward Coke (Instit. iii. 197) supposes them to have been originally the followers of Robert Hood in the reign of Richard the First. See Blackstone's Comm. B. iv. ch. 17."—*Warton, Hist. E. P.* ii. 133; ed. 1824.

77. *lulling—miracles*. For some account of the Miracle Plays, see Massingberd; Hist. Reformation, p. 124; and Hone's Ancient Mysteries. I have little doubt that the particular one here alluded to is "Mystery VIII.," at p. 67 of Hone, about the Miraculous Birth of Christ and the Midwives, the story of which was derived from the Protevangelion, cap. xiv., given in Hone's "Apocryphal Gospels." Compare

> "To pleyes of *miracles*, and mariages."
> *Chaucer, Wyf of Bathes Prologe;* l. 558.

79. *that the lace*, &c. Henry, in his Hist. of Britain, i. 459, says— "Amongst the ancient Britons, when a birth was attended with any difficulty, they put certain girdles made for that purpose about the women in labour, which they imagined gave them immediate and effectual relief. Such girdles were kept with care, till very lately, in many families in the Highlands of Scotland."—*Brand, Pop. Antiq.* ii. 67. This custom seems to have been derived (says Brand) from the Druids. See also a ballad in "The Ballad Book," p. 320. It is easy to see how the friars gladly re-adapted this superstition.

> " For in his male he had a pilwebeer,
> Which that, he saide, was *oure lady veyl.*"
> *Chaucer, Prol.* l. 695.

84. *gold by the eighen*, gold by the eyes. This probably refers to the ornaments of golden net-work worn at this time at the side of the face, thickest just beside the eyes, and which were, in reality, part of the caul. For specimens of them, see Fairholt's Costume in England, pp. 182, 183. So too, *gretehedede* seems to refer to the size of the head-dress. The Wyf of Bath's weighed nearly ten pounds.

89. "Forsoth manye walken, whom I haue seide oft to you, forsoth now and I wepinge seie, the enemyes of Cristis cross, whos ende deeth, *or perisching*, whos god is the wombe, and glorie in confusioun of hem." —*Wycliffe's Bible*, Philip. iii. 18, 19.

91. *slauthe*, sloth. I retain this reading (that of *both* the MSS.), though I have been told that it certainly ought to be *slaughte* = slaughter, because it refers to "whos ende is deeth," quoted in the note above. But the author is not very accurate in quotation, and has already introduced the expression *Such slomerers in slepe*, to which *slauthe* answers well enough. *Sloth* and *Gluttony* are constantly mentioned together by our old writers, as they were the two of the seven deadly sins which seemed most akin; so here, "their *sloth* is their end, and their *gluttony* is their God."

97. *and fele mo othere*, and (so are) many others besides.

100. The error "willen" in MS. A arose from misreading "wiflen," written with two long *esses;* see foot-notes to ll. 233, 531, and 577.

103. *Menures*, Minorites. There was some truth in the Minorites' assertion. They seem to have kept their vows of poverty much more strictly than did the other orders. At first, they settled in the poorer suburbs of crowded towns, among the dregs of the population, and they nursed the patients in the leper hospitals. See the most interesting preface to "Monumenta Franciscana," by J. S. Brewer.

107. Compare the account of friars in Pol. Poems, i. 330;—

> "At the wrastling, and at the wake,
> And chiefe chauntours at the nale (*ale*);

Market-beaters, and *medling* make,
Hoppen and houten with heve and hale," &c.

116. *to coueren with our bones*, to cover our bones with. There are several other instances of this curious position of the word *with* in the poem. See l. 401.

118. *burw3*, a borough; i. e. a large convent. The buildings of the Minorites were, at first, of the meanest and most inexpensive kind; but they gradually began to imitate the other orders.

119. *Chapaile*, chapel. Perhaps the other reading *chapille*, a chapter-house, Lat. *capitulum*, is better.

121. *paynt*, painted; *pulched*, polished.

124. *cnely*, kneel. The infinitive in *y* is common enough.

128. The glazing of windows for convents by rich benefactors seems to have been a favourite way of buying pardons; see Monumenta Franciscana, p. 515; "De Vitratione Fenestrarum." Cf. also *Piers Plowman*, A. iii. 48—62.

Warton's note on this line is—" Your figure kneeling to Christ shall be painted in the great west window. This was the way of representing benefactors in painted glass."—*Hist. Eng. Poet.* ii. 135; ed. 1824.

141. So in Piers Plowman (ed. Wright, p. 189).

" Why menestow thi mood for a mote
In thi brotheres eighe,
Sithen a beem in thyn owene
Ablyndeth thiselve; "

where *menestow* should be *meuestow* = movest thou.

153. *the first*, i. e. the Dominicans, as being the wealthiest, proudest, and most learned. In the next line they are called the *Preachers*.

157. "It was a singular change when the friars began to dwell in palaces and stately houses. . . . Richard Leatherhead, a grey friar from London, having been made bishop of Ossory, in A.D. 1318, pulled down three churches to get materials for his palace. But the conventual buildings, especially of the Black Friars, are described by the author of Pierce Plowman's Creed, a poet of Wycliffe's time, as rivalling the old monasteries in magnificence."—*Massingberd, Hist. Eng. Reform.* p. 119. The following remark on this subject is striking. " Swilk maner of men bigging (*building*) thus biggings semen to turn bred into stones; that is to sey, the bred of the pore, that is, almis beggid, into hepis of stonis, that is, into stonen howsis costly and superflew, and therfor they semen werrar (*worse*) than the fend, that askid stonis into bred."—*Apology attributed to Wycliffe*, p. 49 (Camden Soc.). Compare also,

" Hi domos conficiunt miræ largitatis,
Politis lapidibus, quibusdam quadratis;
Totum tectum tegitur lignis levigatis;
Sed transgressum regulæ probant ista satis.
With an O and an I, facta vestra tabent,
Christus cum sic dixerat, ' foveas vulpes habent.' "
Pol. Poems, p. 255, vol. i.

158. *Say I*, Saw I. We generally find *seʒ* or *seiʒ*. See ll. 208, 421.
159. *Y ʒemede*, I gazed with attention; *ʒerne*, eagerly, earnestly.
161. *knottes*; see Glossary.
165. *posternes in pryuyte*. "These private posterns are frequently alluded to in the reports of the Commissioners for the Dissolution of the Monasteries in the reign of Henry VIII. One of them, speaking of the abbey of Langden, says, 'Wheras immediately descendyng fro my horse, I sent Bartlett your servant, with all my servantes to circumcept the abbay and surely to kepe *all bake dorres and startyng hoilles*, and I myself went alone to the abbottes logeyng joyning upon the feldes and wode, *evyn lyke a cony clapper full of startyng hoilles*.'—(MS. Cotton. Cleop. E. iv. fol. 127.) Another commissioner (MS. Cotton. Cleop. E. iv. fol. 35), in a letter concerning the monks of the Charter-house in London, says, "These charter-howse monkes wolde be called solytary, but to the cloyster dore ther be above xxiiij. keys in the handes of xxiiij. persons, and hit is lyke my letters, unprofytable tayles and tydinges and sumtyme perverse concell commythe and goythe by reason therof. Allso to the buttrey dore ther be xij. sundrye keyes in xij. [mens] hands, wherein symythe to be small husbandrye." Quoted from Mr Wright's notes to the "Crede."
166. *euesed*, bordered. This verb is formed from the A.S. *efese*, the modern English *eaves*, which (it ought to be remembered) is, strictly, a noun in the *singular* number.
167. *entayled*, carved, cut. This word occurs in Spenser, Faerie Queene, Bk. ii. c. 3, st. 27, and c. 6, st. 29.
168. *toten*, to spy; a *tote-hyll* is a hill to spy from, now shortened to Tothill.
169. "The price of a carucate of land, would not raise such another building." Warton's note.
172. *awaytede a woon*, beheld a dwelling; *ybuld*, built.
174. *crochetes*, crockets (see Glossary). They were so named from their resembling bunches or locks of hair, and we find the word used in the latter sense in the Complaint of the Ploughman.

"They kembe her *crokettes* with christall."

Pol. Poems, vol. i. p. 312.

175. *ywritten full thicke*, inscribed with many texts or names.
176. *schapen scheldes*, "coats of arms of benefactors painted in the glass." Warton's note; which see, for examples of them.
177. *merkes of marchauntes*, "their symbols, cyphers, or badges, drawn or painted in the windows. . . Mixed with the arms of their founders and benefactors stand also the *marks* of tradesmen and merchants, who had no arms, but used their marks in a shield like Arms. Instances of this sort are very common."—Warton's note, where he also says they may be found in Great St Mary's, Cambridge, in Bristol cathedral, and in churches at Lynn.
180. *rageman*. Alluding to the Ragman Rolls, originally "a collection of those deeds by which the nobility and gentry of Scotland were

tyrannically constrained to subscribe allegiance to Edward I. of England, in 1296, and which were more particularly recorded in four large rolls of parchment, consisting of 35 pieces, bound together, and kept in the tower of London."—*Jamieson's Scottish Dictionary.* See also Halliwell's Dictionary, where it is explained that several kinds of written rolls, especially those to which many seals were attached, were known by the name of Ragman or Ragman-roll. The modern *rigmarole* is a curious corruption of this term.

181. *tyld opon lofte,* set up on high. It means that the tombs were raised some three or four feet above the ground.

182. *housed in hirnes,* enclosed in corners or niches. The old printed text has *hornes,* for which Warton suggested *hurnes,* and he guessed rightly; but it is odd that he did not observe that MS. B has *hernis,* as he collated the passage with that MS.; besides which, the old *glossary* has *hyrnes,* shewing that *hornes* is a mere misprint.

183. In the church of the Grey Friars, near Newgate, were buried, in all, 663 persons of quality. Stowe says "there were nine tombs of alabaster and marble, invironed with strikes of iron, in the choir." See preface to the "Chronicle of the Grey Friars of London;" (Camden Soc., 1852) p. xxi.

184, 185. MS. A omits these lines, obviously owing to the repetition of *clad for the nones.*

185. "In their *cognisances,* or surcoats of arms."—*Warton.*

188. *gold-beten,* adorned with beaten gold.

194. *peynt til,* painted tiles. MS. B has *paine,* by obvious error for *painte;* the scribe has apparently altered it to *pavine,* thinking it meant *paving.* The old printed text has *poynt til,* on which Warton's note is, "*Point en point* is a French phrase for in order, exactly. This explains the latter part of the line. Or *poynttil* may mean tiles in squares or dies, in chequer-work. See Skinner in POINT, and Du Fresne in PUNCTURA. And then, *ich point after other* will be *one square* after another. So late as the reign of Henry the Eighth, so magnificent a structure as the refectory of Christ-church at Oxford was, at its first building, paved with green and yellow tiles. The whole number was 2600, and each hundred cost 3*s.* 6*d.*" But Warton was slightly misled by the old text; *poynte* merely means *bit, piece,* as in l. 198. It is true that *poynttil* occurs in many dictionaries, glossaries, &c., but *in every case* I find that the *only* quotation given for it is the present line, and I hold it to be a *mere misprint. Peynt* = painted is common enough (see l. 192), but I doubt the existence of *poynt* in the sense of *pointed* or *squared.* Indeed, Mr Ellis, rejecting Warton's explanation, proposed to explain *poynttil* by *pantiles,* which, however, cannot be used for paving, not being *flat.*

"And yit, God wot, unnethe the foundement
Parformed is, ne of oure *pavyment*
Is nought a *tyle* yit withinne our wones."
Chaucer, Sompnoures Tale, l. 403.

197. I trow the produce of the land in a great shire would not furnish

that place (hardly) one bit towards the other end ; a stronger phrase than "from one end to the other," as Warton explains it. *Oo* properly = one.

199. *Chaptire-hous.* "The chapter-house was magnificently constructed in the style of church-architecture, finely vaulted, and richly carved."—*Warton.*

201. With " a seemly ceiling, or roof, very lofty."—*Warton.*

202. *y-pcynted*, painted. Before tapestry became fashionable, the walls of rooms were painted. For proofs, see Warton's long note.

203. *fraytour*, refectory.

209. *chymneyes*, fireplaces. Langlande complains bitterly that the rich often despise dining in the hall, and eat by themselves "in a privy parlour, or in a chamber with a chimney." *Piers Plowman:* ed. Wright, p. 179, vol. i.

211. *dortour*, dormitory.

212. *fermery*, infirmary ; *fele mo*, many more. Chaucer uses *fermerere* for the person who had charge of the infirmary.—*Sompnoures Tale*, l. 151 ; *dortour* occurs in the same passage, just 4 lines above.

216. Compare

" Yif us a busshel whet, or malt, or reye,
A Goddes kichil, or a trip of chese,
Or elles what yow list, we may not chese," &c.
Sompnoures Tale, l. 38.

217. *onethe*, with difficulty.

219. *ytoted*, investigated, espied.

220. Friars are also accused of fatness in the following :—

" I have lyued now fourty ȝers
And fatter men about the neres
Ȝit sawe I neuer then are thes frers
In coutreys ther thai rayke.
Meteles, so *megre* are thai made, and penaunce so *puttes ham doun*
That ichone is an *hors-lade*, whan he shal trusse of toun ! "[1]
Pol. Poems, i. 264.

222. "With a face as fat as a full bladder that is blown quite full of breath ; and it hung like a bag on both his cheeks, and his chin lolled (or flapped) about with a jowl (or double-chin) that was as great as a goose's egg, grown all of fat ; so that all his flesh wagged about like a quick mire (quagmire)."

228. The line " with double worsted well ydight " occurs in the Complaint of the Ploughman ; *Pol. Poems*, i. 334.

229. The *kirtle* was the under-garment, which was worn *white* by the Black Friars. The outer *black* garment is here called the *cope*. The *kirtle* was white, and good enough in its *ground* (texture) to admit

---

[1] *nores*, kidneys ; compare Ger. *Niere*. Of course, the expressions "meteles" and "megre" are ironical. *Rayke*, wander about ; cf. l. 72 of the " Crede ; " *hors-lade*, a horse-load ; *trusse of toun*, pack off out of the town. The same passage is in Monumenta Franciscana, p. 602.

of being dyed in *grain* (of a fast colour). The kirtle " appears to have been a kind of tunic or surcoat, and to have resembled the hauberk or coat of mail; it seems in some instances to have been worn next the shirt, if not to serve the purpose of it, and was also used as an exterior garment by pages when they waited on the nobility."—*Strutt, Dress and Habits*, 349. When Jane Shore did penance, she was "out of all array save her *kirtle* only."—*Holinshed*, p. 1135; ed. 1577.

233. The mistake "willen" in MS. A arose from misreading "wiffen." See note to l. 100.

242. *euelles*, evil-less; but there seems little force in this epithet, and I feel sure the reading is corrupt. The other readings are no better.

247. "It is merely a pardoner's trick; test and try it!"

252. An allusion to the reputation of the Dominicans for scholastic learning.

256. "Three popes, John XXI., Innocent V., and Benedict XI., were all taken from the order of Black Friars, between A.D. 1276-1303."

Massingberd, Eng. Ref., p. 117.

263. *in lyknes*, by way of parable.

268. The spelling *angerlich* is the correct one; compare

"The kings law wol no man deme
Angerliche without answere."

Comp. of Ploughm. Pol. Poems, i. 323.

271. *creatour*, creature.

274. "That fully follow the faith, as the gospels tell us, apart from fables, and from mystifications of paraphrases and glosses. For the meaning of *glose*, compare

" I have to day ben at your chirche at messe,
And sayd a sermoun *after my simple wit*,
Nought al *after the text of holy wryt*.
For it is *hard* for yow, as I suppose,
And therfor wil I teche yow ay the *glose*.
Glosyng is a ful glorious thing certayn,
For letter sleth, so as we clerkes sayn."

Chaucer, Somp. Tale, l. 80.

276. *byhyght*, promised.

280. *I madde*, I grow mad; cf. l. 41.

282. *good*, property, here and elsewhere.

283. *catell*, wealth.

285. The spellings *vsun, vsune, vson* are all bad.

287. "Do naught but proffer them privately a penny for saying a mass, and put out my eye *if his lad is not ready* to take it." The reading of the old printed copy, "but his *name* be *Prest*," i. e. *if his name be not Priest*, is very absurd. The *knaue* or lad is the man who followed the begging friars about to carry their earnings.

" A stourdy harlot (*fellow*) ay went hem byhynde,
That was her hostis man, and bar a sak,

And what men yaf hem, layd it on his bak."
Sompnoure's Tale, l. 46.

291. "As towching our habite and clothinge, yt is ordeyned that the breddithe of the hode pas not the sholder-boone, and that the lenghte therof pas not the coorde behinde; and the lenghte of the habit shalle nat pas the lenkithe of hym that werethe yt, and the breddith therof haue nat past xvi. spannys at the most, nor les then xiiij., but-yf the gretnes of the brodre require more after the mynd of the warden, and the lenghte of the slevis shall cum over the vtter joynt of the finger and no further. And the brethern may haue mantellis of vyle and course clothe, not curiusly made or pynched aboute the necke, nat towching the grauud by a hole spanne." General Statutes of the Gray Friars; Mon. Francisc. p. 575. For pictures of the friars' dresses see Dugdale's Monasticon, last edition.

292. "More cloth is folded in cutting his cope than was in St Francis's frock, when he first established the order."

296. The *cote*, worn under the *cope*, was of fur; but it was cut short at the knee, and craftily buttoned close, lest it should be perceived by the stricter brethren.

298. Among the "articles that Pope Clement saithe that the Bretherne [Franciscans] be bownde to kepe vnder payne of dedly synne," the second is, "that the bretherne shalle were no shone."—*Mon. Franc.*, p. 572. At p. 28 of Mon. Franc. there is a story of one Walter de Madele, a Franciscan of Oxford, who found a pair of shoes and went to matins in them; he dreamt the next night that he was attacked by thieves, and putting out his feet to *show that he was a friar*, found to his confusion that he was shod. Starting up from bed, he throws his shoes out of the window.

299. *for bleynynge*, to prevent blains on their heels.

300. *yhamled*, cut short at the ancle, so that people should not easily see that they had hose on; such was their crafty device.

301. "And spices scattered loose in their purses (bags), to give away where they liked." Compare

"And also many a dyuers spyse
In bagges about thai bere.
Al that for women is plesaud,
Ful redy certes have thai;
But lytel gyfe thai the husband,
That for al shal pay."—*Pol. Poems*, i. 265

The friars used to bribe the fair wives, to get their good word, thus "throwing away a sprat to catch a whale." See Chaucer, Prol. 233; Somp. Tale, 94—101.

303. *knewen men*, if men knew; cf. l. 770. The old reading, *knowen*, is clearly wrong.

304. *nought but*, only; cf. prov. Eng. *nobbut*.

308. *heremita*, not *heremite*, is the true reading; it is a quotation from Piers Plowman (ed. Wright, p. 312);

"Poul *primus heremita*
Hadde parroked hymselve," &c.

For the story of Paul of Thebes who, during the persecution under Decius, fled to a desert on the East of the Nile, and there became the founder of the anchorites or solitary hermits, see Mrs Jameson's Sacred and Legendary Art, vol. II. p. 368.

311. *Forto,* until. The Carmelites lived as hermits till the Franciscans betook themselves to the poor suburbs of towns; so says their apologist.

324. The alliteration is very defective; it is perhaps eked out by a very strong emphasis on *thou* and *thiselfe.*

326. "Thou shalt (at the next meeting of the chapter) have a letter of fraternization granted you, duly sealed." Massingberd says (p. 118) —"Another marvellous way, by which the rich were brought in to share all the graces of poverty, without practising its privations, was by *conventual letters,* or charters of fraternization; by which the person presented with them was entitled to all the benefit of the prayers, masses, and meritorious deeds of the order." Compare

"Ye sayn me thus, *how that I am your brother:*
Ye, certes, (quod the frere), trusteth wel;
I toke our dame the *letter,* under our *sel.*"
Somp. Tale, 1. 426.

328. *prouinciall,* one who has the direction of the several convents of a *province.*

336. *preyinge of synne,* sinful praying.

341. A omits *s* in *aisliche;* but the reading of B (*aillich*) shews that the original had *aifliche,* f being again confused with *l,* as at 1. 100.

342. *on leuest,* believest in.

345. *halt,* boldeth; so we find *rit* for rideth, *fynt* for findeth, &c.

347. *letten but werchen,* prevent him from working.

350. *For thei ben,* whether they be; *on to trosten,* to trust in.

351. "I would requite thee with thy reward, according to my power."

355. "They are as disdainful as Lucifer, that (for his pride) falls from heaven." Perhaps we should read *droppede.*

356. "With their hearts (full) of haughtiness, (see) how they hallow churches, and deal in divinity as dogs treat bones."

358. "He had i-made many a fair *mariage.*" *Chaucer, Prol.* 1. 212.

360. In the Complaint of the Ploughman, it is said of the Pope that

"He maketh bishops for *earthly thanke,*
And no thing at all for Christ[e]s sake."
Pol. Poems, vol. i. p. 315.

The context shews that *earthly thanke* means a *bribe.*

361. "They wish for honours:—only look at their deeds (and you'll see proofs of it)."

362. I have no doubt, from the context, that these goings-on of the

friars at Hertford mean that they cajoled Richard II. and his relatives into granting them money. There was no house of the Black Friars at Hertford itself (there was one of Black *Monks*), but the allusion is doubtless to their famous convent at King's Langley, in Hertfordshire, the richest (says Dugdale) in all England. Richard II. made no less than three grants to it, and it received large sums from Edmund de Langley (who was born in that town), and from Edmund's first wife. "And 'tis said that this great Lady, having been somewhat wanton in her younger years, became an *hearty Penitent*, and departed this life *anno* 1394. 17 R. II. and was *buried in this church*" (the church of the Black Friars' convent); *Chauncy's Hertfordsh.*, p. 545. Edmund de Langley was also buried here, and so was the king himself. The custom was, to bequeath one's body to a convent for burial, and to bequeath a large sum of money to it at the same time ; see ll. 408—417. It should be noted, too, that Richard often held a royal Christmas at Langley ; he did so certainly in 1392, and again in 1394 ; see Stow's and Capgrave's Chronicles. This, doubtless, gave the Friars excellent opportunities.

365. See Glossary, s. v. Claweþ.

366. "God grant they lead them well, in heavenly living, and cajole them not for their own advantage, to the peril of their (the kings') souls."

374. *lefte*, remained.

375. *digne*, disdainful ; hence, repulsive ; but there is not often much logical sequence or connection in proverbs of this sort. Yet that this is the right explanation is evident from Chaucer ; see the Glossary.

378. *Als as*, all so as, i. e. just as if.

379. *leesinges lyeth*, lie their lies.

383. See note to l. 29. The friar in the Sompnoures Tale seems to have been a Carmelite ; see Somp. T. l. 416.

387. *by lybbeth*, live by.

388. "We know of no subtlety, Christ knows the truth."

393. *And*, if.

401. *to wynnen withe my fode*, to earn my food with.

402. *lerne*, teach ; common in prov. English.

405. Catus amat pisces, sed non vult tingere plantam.

406. *so—parted*, are not given away in that manner.

409. Carefully compare the death-bed scene described fully in Massingberd's Eng. Ref. pp. 165—168; and see also Chaucer's Sompnoures Tale.

> "Si dives in patria quisquis infirmetur,
> Illuc frater properans et currens monetur ;
> Et statim cum venerit infirmo loquetur,
> Ut cadaver mortuum fratribus donetur."
> *Pol. Poems*, vol. i. p. 257.

414. *Anuell;* see Glossary.

415. "It is God's forbidding but that she die while she is in a mind to share her wealth among us ; God let her live no longer, for our letters (of confraternity) are so numerous." It was of course inconvenient that those who had obtained these letters should live long afterwards.

421. "I saw a simple man hang upon (bend over) his plough."

I here venture to quote the *whole* of the *Prologue* to the Ploughman's Tale, from an early undated edition. It is much to the point, and was omitted by Mr Wright when reprinting the Plowman's Tale itself.

"Here endeth the Manciples tale, and here beginneth the Plowmannes Prologue.

> The Plowman plucked vp his plowe
>   Whan Midsomer Moone was comen in,
> And saied his bestes shuld eate inowe,
>   And lige in the Grasse vp to the chin.
> Thei been feble bothe Oxe and Cowe,
>   Of hem nis left but bone and skinne,
> He shoke of her shere and coulter ofdrowe,
>   And honged his harnis on a pinne.
>
> He toke his tabarde and his staffe eke,
>   And on his hedde he set his hat,
> And saied he would sainct Thomas seke,
>   On pilgremage he goth forth plat.
> In scrippe he bare bothe bread and lekes,
>   He was forswonke and all forswat;
> Men miȝt haue sen through both his chekes,
>   And euery wang-toth and where it sat.
>
> Our hoste behelde well all about,
>   And sawe this men was Sunne ibrent,
> He knewe well by his senged snout,
>   And by his clothes that were to-rent,
> He was a man wont to walke about,
>   He nas not alwaie in cloister ipent;
> He could not religiousliche lout,
>   And therefore was he fully shent.
>
> Our hoste him axed, 'what man art thou?'
>   'Sir' (q*uod* he) 'I am an hine;
> For I am wont to go to the plow,
>   And earne my meate er [1] that I dine;
> To swette and swinke I make auowe,
>   My wife and children therewith to finde;
> And serue God and I wist how,
>   But we leude men been full blinde.
>
> For clerkes saie we shullen be fain
>   For her liuelod swette and swinke,
> And thei right nought vs giue again,
>   Neither to eate ne yet to drinke.

---

[1] Old *copy*, "yer."

> Thei mowe by lawe, as thei sain,
>   Vs curse and dampne to hell[e] brinke;
> Thus thei putten vs to pain
>   With candles queint and belles clinke.
>
> Thei make vs thralles at her lust,
>   And sain we mowe not els be saued;
> Thei haue the corne and we the dust,
>   Who speaketh there-again, thei saie he raued.
>   [*Four lines lost.*]
>
> 'What? man,' (qu*od* our hoste) 'canst thou preache?
>   Come nere and tel vs some holy thing.'
> 'Sir,' qu*od* he, 'I heard ones teache
>   A priest in pulpit a good preaching.'
> 'Saie one,' qu*od* our hoste, 'I thee beseche.'
>   'Sir, I am redy at your bidding;
> I praie you that no man me reproche,
>   While that I am my tale telling.'

Thus endeth the Prologue, and here foloweth the first parte of the tale."

425. It means that his shoes were so worn and ill-made that, whilst his toes peeped out, his hose overhung his gaiters (*hokschynes* = *hoskins*), and so got bedaubed with mud. See *Hoeshins* in Jamieson.

428. *as mete*, as tight, or scanty, as the shoes were. It is the A.S. *mǣte*, middling, mean. It being a hard word, the scribe of MS. B erased it, and the old printer misprinted it.

431. *worthen*, become. The wrong reading *worthi* may have been an error in the old original text, from which texts A, B, and C are all derived. In Layamon's "Brut" the past participle of the verb *worthen*, to become, takes the forms iwurðen, iwurden, iworðen, iworþe; and is sometimes used in the exact sense here required, as in —"for alle ure heðene-scipe hæne is iwurðen"—"for all our heathendom is become base."—*Layamon*, vol. 2, p. 279.

432. *reufull*, sorry-looking; a great improvement on the old reading *rentfull*.

436. Compare—"As two of them [Minorites] were going into a neighbouring wood, picking their way along the rugged path over the frozen mud and rigid snow, whilst the blood lay in the track of their naked feet without their perceiving it," &c.—*Mon. Franc.* p. 632.

437. *laye*; the old printed text has *lath*; this is because the printer misread *laye* as *laþe*.

443. "At heiȝ prime perkyn · lette þe plouȝ stonde."—*Piers Pl.* A. vii. 105.

445. "If livelihood (i. e. means of living) fail thee, I will lend thee such wealth as God hath sent; come, dear brother." *Go we* (= come along) was a common exclamation; cf. "go we dyne, gowe," Piers Pl. A. *prol.* 105.

452. "For there I expected to have known (it)."

456. "Attendite a falsis prophetis, qui veniunt ad vos *in vestimentis ovium*, intrinsecus autem sunt lupi rapaces." Mat. vii. 15 (Vulgate).

459. *werwolves*, lit. man-wolves, Fr. *loupgarous*, from the Teutonic *wer*, a man, which was modified into *gar* in Norman-French. For a full discussion of the etymology, see Glossary to Sir F. Madden's edition of "William and the Werwulf," a re-issue of which I am now preparing for the E. E. T. S. For a full discussion of the very prevalent mediæval superstition, that men could be turned into peculiarly ferocious wolves, see "A Book on Werwolves," by S. Baring Gould, and Thorpe's Northern Mythology.

462. *Curates*, parish-priests with a cure of souls. The friars were continually interfering with and opposing them.

"——unnethe may prestes seculers
Gete any service, for thes frers," &c.
Pol. Poems, i. 267.

468. *confessions*, i. e. the right of hearing confessions, and being paid for so doing.

469. *sepultures*, burials. They used to get people to order in their wills that they should be buried in a convent-church, and then they would be paid for the singing of masses for them.

471. *he loketh*, they look for, look out for.

477. "I trow that some wicked wight wrought these orders through the subtlety of the tale called Golias; or else it was Satan," &c. A satire on the monkish orders, called *Apocalypsis Goliæ*, may be found among the poems by Walter Mapes, &c., edited by Mr Wright for the Camden Society. The idea expressed in l. 479 is this:—perhaps, after all, that satire of Golias was written as an artful contrivance for bringing about the disrepute of the monks, and the rise of the mendicant orders. It is certain that the friars succeeded at first because the monks had become so dissolute, but it is not likely that this particular poem had much to do with it. *Gleym* = bird-lime, and hence subtlety, craft, guile. It is a strong metaphor, but explained by our author's own words in l. 564; "I liken it to a limed twig, to draw men to hell."

486. Cain's name was generally spelt *Caim* or *Caym* in Early English: whence Wycliffe declared that the letters C, A, I, M meant the Carmelites, Augustines, Jacobins, and Minorites, and he delighted in calling the convents "Caim's castles," an idea which appears below, at l. 559. It was common to call wicked people Cain's children or Judas's children; see Piers Pl. A. *prol.* 35, and x. 149.

"Nou se the sothe whedre it be swa,
That frere Carmes come of a K,
The frer Austynes come of A,
Frer Jacobynes of I,
Of M comen the frer Menours;
Thus grounded *Caym* thes four ordours

That fillen the world ful of errours,
And of ypocrisy."—*Pol. Poems*, i. 266.

487. The Wycliffites were never tired of comparing the friars to *Pharisees ;* ll. 487—502 and 546—584 are entirely devoted to this comparison. This comparison, and the one in l. 456, are both found in the Apology attributed to Wycliffe. *feyned for gode,* feigned to be good men. The old printed text has "Sarysenes, feyned for God."

489. *kynde ypocrites,* natural hypocrites, hypocrites by nature.

492. *wo worthe you,* wo happen to you; *worthe* is the imperative of *wurthen,* to become, to happen.

498. Cf. note to l. 574.

499. Cf. note to l. 554.

503. "Her *(their)* high maister is Beliall."—*Pol. Poems,* i. 310.

507. Cf. note to l. 462.

510. The old reading *dernlich,* secretly, gives no sense; *deruelich* means laboriously, industriously. Thus in Allit. Poems (ed. Morris, E. E. T. S.), p. 56, l. 632, Abraham tells his servant to seethe a kid, "And he *deruely,* at his dome, dy3t hyt bylyue;" and he industriously, at his bidding, got it ready soon.

516. *vnteyned,* bad spelling for *vntyned,* unfastened. It occurs in this sense in the following: "næs þær duru *ontyned,* ne woall to-slyten, ne eah-þyrl geopened;" there was no door *unfastened,* nor wall rent through, nor window opened. MS. C.C.C. 196, p. 43

518. *bare,* barren.

521. *pouere in gost,* poor in spirit. "Gostly pouert is sum tyme wan a thing hath litil of sum spirit; and thus was Crist most pore, for he had lest of the spirit of prid."—*Apology attributed to Wycliffe,* p. 41; cf. Sompnoures Tale, l. 215.

523. *Proue hem,* i. e. try the experiment of proving them.

528. For a brief summary of Wycliffe's charges against the friars, see Massingberd, Eng. Ref., p. 139; or consult Lewis's or Le Bas' life of Wycliffe; or, better still, Wycliffe's own Two treatises against the Friars, edited by James; 4to, Oxford, 1608. He died Dec. 31, 1384, at Lutterworth.

532. To *lolle* properly means, to profess the doctrines of Wycliffe; and "oueral *lollede* him" = especially accused him of *lolling.* See the poem against the Lollards, in Pol. Poems, ii. 245, where we find

"And, parde, *lolle* thei never so longe,
Yut wol lawe make hem lowte;"

and again, "double dethe for suyche *lollynge.*" A *loller* means a sluggard, an idle vagabond; see Piers Plowman (ed. Wright), pp. 514, 527. In the Complaint of the Ploughman the term is applied, not to the *Wycliffites,* but to the *friars,* who are "Icleped *lollers* and londlese;" *Pol. Poems,* i. 305. At the same time, the term *Lollard* was freely applied to the so-called heretics, and had been used in Germany as early as 1309. The latter word was probably formed from Ger. *lullen* or *lullen*, to stammer, mumble (Ducange gives " Lollaerd, *mussitator*,") but the two words *loller* and *Lollard* were *purposely* confused, to the no small perplexity of modern inquirers.

536. " If you can find four friars in one convent that follow that rule, why, then, I've lost all my powers of tasting, touching, and testing."

538—545. In *all* former editions, these lines have been rendered mere nonsense by the absurd insertion of a full stop at the end of l. 543. But the construction is just the same as in ll. 536-7; and the sentence is framed in the same ironical strain. It means, " Only find fault with them ever so little, and blame their mode of life, and if he does not leap up on high in hardness of heart, and at once call you a thing of naught, and revile your name openly with proud words that transgress his rule, both with 'thou liest' and again 'thou liest,' in his haughtiness of soul, and turn about like a tyrant that torments himself—*if he does not do this, why then I'll admit that* a lord is more loath to give to a knave than to such a begging friar as he is, though he be the best in the town." In other words, " we know that a lord would rather give to a knave than to a friar; but, if my words be not true, consider the order of all things as inverted, and that a lord is *more loath* to give to a knave than to a friar." Such a construction is difficult to explain on paper, but a good reader would bring out the force of it easily enough.

550. *chapolories*, scapulars. The writer cleverly substitutes the *scapulars* of the friars for the *phylacteries* of the Pharisees. The scapular (Fr. *scapulaire*, Ital. *scapulare*) was so called because thrown over the shoulders. Compare the words of Jack Upland—" What betokeneth your great hood, your *scaplerie*, your knotted girdle, and your wide cope ? "— *Pol. Poems*, ii. 19. This word has been queerly misunderstood; Richardson thought it meant a *chapelry*, and inserted this line in his dictionary under " Chapel." But the spellings *scoplory* and *scapelary* are both given in the Promptorium Parvulorum, and the alteration into *chapolory* is less remarkable than the spelling of *chaff* in l. 663, viz. *schaf;* and see note to l. 684.

554. Compare

" Priestes should for no catell plede,
   But chasten hem in charitè;
Ne to no battaile should men lede,
   For inhaunsing of her own degree;
Nat wilue sittings in high see,
   No soueraignty in house ne hall;
All wordly worship defie and flee;
   For who willeth highnes, foule shal fall."
            Ploughman's Complaint, Pol. Poems, i. 306.

559. See note to l. 486.

564. So in Piers Plowman (ed. Wright), p. 170—" For lecherie in likynge is lyme-yerd of helle."

569. *her propre*, their own.

571. " Except money may make measure of (i. e. may moderate) the

pain, according as his power of payment is,—his penance shall fail; and God grant it be a *good* help (i. e. a *heavy* payment) for the health of the souls."

574. "Now *maister* (quod this lord) I yow biseke.—
No *maister*, sir (quod he) but servitour,
Though I have had in scole such honour.
God likith not that *Raby* men us calle
Neyther in market, neyther in your large halle."
Sompnoures Tale, l. 484.

So too in the Comp. of the Ploughman; Pol. Poems, i. 337.

577. The sense is carried on from *forʒetten this* to *Wher* in l. 579. "Friars have forgotten this, viz. whether Francis," &c.

583. *and—liste*, and choose when it suits him; meaning, I suppose, that he chooses his own hours for service, &c.

586. "He touches not the text itself, but takes it to found his glosses on."

591. *Stumlen in tales*, flounder about in his legends of the saints, instead of preaching God's word.

593. "And look out (find out) for themselves lying stories, such as please the people."

597. *a lymitour*; see Chaucer, Prol. l. 209. "It was, of course, however, necessary to regulate the system of begging alms. . . . This was effected by assigning districts to each convent, within which its members were to take their rounds, and generally each individual friar had his own limits prescribed; whence the name that was commonly given to them of *limitors*. When the system was established, the alms of bread, bacon, and cheese, logs of wood for their fire, and other ordinary gifts, were ready for the friar when he called." *Massingberd, Eng. Ref.* p. 110.

603. *Wherto*, wherefore, answering to *But for* in l. 605.

608. The old printer, misreading Y as þ, and supposing þ to stand for *þe* or *þei*, turned *Y-cloped* into Thei clothed.

610. *onlie*, singularly, in a way peculiar to themselves, "neither in order nor out," as we read in l. 45; cf. also l. 534.

613. *for*, before.

614. *claþ*, cloth. The adjective *pur*, pure, clean, shews that *cloth* is meant; besides, they would not be put in *clay* when "*near* dead," but only *after* death. The mis-reading *clay* in A is easily explained; the writer simply mistook þ to mean *y*, just as, by a common blunder, y^e and y^t occur often in C for *the* and *that*. The reading *cleye* in B is due to the same thing, only that here the scribe also changed the spelling at his own good pleasure, as he has very unwisely done throughout the MS. The announcement in this line that friars, when near dead, were wrapped up in white cloth, and had *pots put on their heads*, is strange and startling, and a reference to l. 627 seems to shew that there existed a system of disposing of useless friars by a process not very different from suffocation; but it would be desirable to have more light thrown upon this passage from other sources. A request for further explanation was

inserted in Notes and Queries, 3rd S. xi. p. 277, but has elicited, as yet, no reply.

623. " Or maimed by accident, or sick lepers." The old text has *mayned* for *maymed*, and *lyke* for *syke*, a mistake due to reading the long *s* (f) as an *l*, as in ll. 100, 233, and 341.

626. " Except he beg his bread, his bed is got ready for him ; he shall be put under a pot in a secret chamber so that he shall not live or last long after." Cf. ll. 614, 732.

631. " But whosoever hath scoffed at a friar," &c.

633. " It were as good for him to have displeased a wealthy lord."

635. *compased his morther*, contrived his murder ; the old printed text has *mother ;* had the author meant *mother*, he would have written *moder ;* see l. 2.

636. "Than if he had bestowed a buffet on a begging friar."

641. *this*, this law ; *an other*, another law.

642. " That which they catch hold of, they hold tight, [and] soon hide it away."

643, 644. Difficult ; but the meaning seems to be—" Their hearts are fully hid (from the world's wealth) in their high cloisters—quite as much as curs abstain from refuse carrion ! " In other words, they *no more* devote their minds to contemplation and abstain from coveting, than a dog abstains from carrion.

648, 649. The reading *wilfuller* (of MS. B) gives the right *sense ;* the readings *wilfullok(e)r* and *folloke* are easily accounted for by remembering that the old spelling of *wilfuller* would be *wilfulloker*, just as *lightloker* (= lightlier), *sadloker* (= sadder), and many other such comparative forms, occur continually in old authors, as, e. g. in Piers Plowman. The *wil* was dropped in the old printed text because the *repetition* of it looked wrong, and the final *r*, which may have been obscurely written, went with it. The sense is ; "just test their soberness, and you may soon know that no wasp in the world will sting more fiercely, [than they will sting you] for stepping on the toe of a stinking friar." But there is probably a line lost between ll. 648 and 649.

655. *pursut of*, prosecution (of heretics) by.

657. *Wat* is no doubt the right reading ; the reading *Water* arose from adding *er*, and forgetting to put in the *l*. *Wat* is the common form, and was a very common name ; cf. Piers Plowman, A. v. 30. Walter Brute was a Welsh gentleman, who called into question the doctrines of the power of the keys, auricular confession, pardons, &c., and declared that pretended miracles ought to be carefully examined into. In particular he protested, Oct. 15, 1391, against the condemnation, for heresy, of William Swinderby ; on Jan. 19, 1391-2, he confessed to having communicated with the said heretic ; on Friday, Oct. 3, 1393, he appeared before the bishop of Hereford, who had prosecuted him unceasingly, for final trial, and on the succeeding Monday, Oct. 6, he submitted himself to the same, not without having well defended many of his opinions. A long account of his defence will be found in Foxe's Acts and Monuments,

vol. 3, pp. 131—188 (ed. Cattley, 1841). Fuller speaks of Walter Brute as one of the "Worthies of Wales."

659. I venture to read *hym*, as the sense requires; *hem* must have been copied from the line above. Brute having submitted himself to the bishop, the friars partly failed in their object; but they still tell men, says our author, that he is a heretick, and go on preaching against him. This use of the present tense helps greatly to fix the date of the poem in 1394. Compare the account of William Swinderby in Massingberd's Eng. Ref. p. 172.

660. Compare
"Whoso speketh ayenst her powere,
It shal be holden heresie."
Compl. Ploughm., *Pol. Poems*, i. 329.

663. Imitated from Piers Plowman, A. i. 167,
" *Chewen* heore *charite*, and chiden after more!"
So here, "They gobble down their charity as hounds do bran," and no more is seen of it. *Schaf*, chaff; prob. put for *bran*, with which dogs used to be commonly fed. Notes and Queries, 3rd S. xi. 191.

664. *passen pursutes*, exceed all other persecutions, i. e. they both wish to murder men's souls after burning their bodies, and they would do it too! A Wicliffite is threatened with the words,
' Thou shalt be brent in balefull fire,
And all thy sect I shall destrie."—*Pol. Poems*, i. 341.
Men were sometimes burnt for heresy before the year 1401. See Wyclif's Works, ed. Arnold, i. x.

670. "They nold nat demen after the face."—*Compl. Ploughm., Pol. Poems*, i. 325.

681. "*Possessioneres*, i. e. the regular orders of *monks*, who possessed landed property and enjoyed rich revenues. The *friars* were forbidden by their rule to possess property, which they only did under false pretences; they depended for support on voluntary offerings."—*Cant. Tales*, ed. Wright, p. 82, *foot-note*.
" Suche annuels has made thes frers
So wely and so gay,
That ther may no *possessioners*
Mayntene thair array."—*Pol. Poems*, i. 267.

684. I venture to read *chesen*. The original text probably had *schesen*, altered in MS. A to *schosen*. The strange spelling *schesen* is paralleled by *schaf* for *chaf*, and *chuldest* for *schuldest* in l. 124.

691. *Aldermen*, an allusion to the twenty-four elders, Rev. iv. 4; we read " et mittebant coronas suas *ante thronum* " in ver. 10 (Vulgate).

695. Alluding to the dress of the Dominicans; see note to l. 29.

703. "I suppose this refers to St Hildegardis, a nun who flourished in the middle of the twelfth century, and who was celebrated among the Roman Catholics as a prophetess. Her prophecies are not uncommon in manuscripts, and they have been printed. Those which relate to the

future corruptions in the monkish orders are given in Foxe's Acts and Monuments, book vi., and in other works."—Mr Wright's note to this line. St Hildegarde was abbess of St Rupert's mount, near Bingen; born A.D. 1098, died in 1180. See Neander's Church History, vii. 291-5 (ed. Torrey).

705. Cf. note to l. 468. Innocent III. made confession compulsory, once a year at least.

710. *after vsed*, (perhaps) used after, i. e. followed after, held to, practised accordingly. But it is an awkward expression.

713. So in Piers Plowman, A. viii. 3, "And purchasede him a pardoun *A pena et a culpa*." Such was the usual phrase.

716. "And they deal with loans and biddings;" see Gloss. s. v. *lone* and *bode*.

719. Alludes to the Franciscans; gray was the original colour of their habit, but after a time dark-brown was introduced. "On St George's day, 1502, they relinquished the *London russet* which they had for some time worn, and resumed the undyed white-grey which had been their original habit."—*Greyfriar's Chronicle, Pref.*, p. xiv.

724. *biggen* may either mean *buy*, or *construct*.

725. *And als*, and according as.

729. *furste-froyt*, first-fruits. Cf. Sompnoures Tale, l. 577.

738. *scon*, better spelt *schon*, shoes. The old text has *stone!* Sc and St are often hardly distinguishable in MSS.

744. 'Now must each cobbler set his son to school.'

748. *bychop*, bishop. The alliteration requires this word, but the old printed text has *abbot*. Such an alteration must have been made by the printer *of set purpose*. Compare

"For to lords they woll be liche,
An harlots sonne not worth an hawe!"
Pol. Poems, i. 312.

750. Compare

"Lords also mote to them loute," &c.
Pol. Poems, i. 308.

758. *faytoures*. Mr Wright's edition has *forytoures*, which he supposes a mistake in the old text. But *forytoures* is an error of *his* printer, for all three of the other editions have *faytoures*, as in the MSS.

761. "No one could sit down to meat, high or low, but he must ask a friar or two, who when they came would play the host to themselves, and carry away bread and meat besides."—*qu. in Massingberd, Eng. Ref.*, p. 110.

763. *randes*, strips, slices. The old text has *bandes*. This improves the alliteration, but it does not appear that there is any such word. See Glossary.

764. Compare

"With chaunge of many manner meates,
With song and solas sitting long," &c.
Pol. Poems, i. 307.

769. "Fitzralph, in his *Apology at Avignon*, accused them of 'philosophising' in the chambers of the most beautiful maidens; and Eccleston says, that even so early as his time, Friar Walter of Reigate confessed that these familiarities were one of the ways by which the foul fiend vexed the order."—*Mossingberd, Eng. Ref.*, p. 110. Cf. Piers Plowman (ed. Wright), p. 445. And the following—

"Iche man that here shal lede his life,
That has a faire doghter or a wyfe,
Be-war that no frer ham shryfe,
Nauther loud nor stille."—*Pol. Poems*, i. 265.

771. *homly*, familiarly. Mr Wright has *holy*.
777. *Helye*, Elias.
782. "have laid it in water," i. e. drowned it, sunk it. *Hire* is used because *rewle* is feminine.
784. *Ne were*, If it were not for.
785. Compare

"Had they been out of religion,
They must have hanged at the plowe,
Threshing and diking fro toune to toune
With sorrie meat, and not halfe ynowe."
Pol. Poems, i. 335.

808. When Christ descended into hell, he fetched out Adam and the patriarchs, and led them with him to heaven. This was called the Harrowing of Hell; the story is given in the apocryphal gospel of Nicodemus, and is repeated at great length in Piers Plowman.

810. *stei3*, ascended.

816. *generall*, i. e. Catholic, universal. So in p. 1 of the Apology attributed to Wycliffe, we find the "*general feith*," meaning the Catholic faith.

817—821. These five lines are *certainly spurious*. They are in neither of the MSS., and are found only in the old printed copy. The reason for inserting them was a wish to conceal the fact that five lines had been *suppressed* which *are* found in *both* the MSS.; viz., ll. 822, 823, and 828—830, and which are now printed *for the first time*. The reason for suppressing them was that they appear to contain the doctrine of transubstantiation, and as the object of printing the book at all was to attack the Romish party, it would never have done to retain these lines. Hence ll. 817—821 were forged; but the forger of them, though he has given us five lines which imitate the author's style very ingeniously, did not truly understand the laws of alliterative verse, and formed ll. 817—819 on a wrong principle, putting *two* of the rime-letters into the *second* half of the line, and only *one* into the *first* half, whereas the usual practice is the contrary to this. True, lines of this type *do* occur, as e. g. at l. 26, but they are very rare, and only admissible as a variation. To allow *three* such lines to follow each other is against all ordinary usage. But this is not the only difficulty. There is really *no place* where ll. 817—

821 can properly come in. To insert them where I have done involves the absurdity of putting *Amen* in the middle of a sentence; whilst to insert them any where else only makes matters still worse. Again, the suppression of the genuine lines rendered ll. 824—827 and ll. 831—839 meaningless, and I will venture to say that no one has hitherto been able to make out to what they can possibly refer. But the mystery is now cleared up; they discuss the doctrine of *transubstantiation*.

822. "And I believe in the sacrement too, that the very God is in both flesh and blood fully, who suffered death for us." *Sacremens* (MS. A) should be *sacrement*, as in MS. B. *On* = upon, in; A.S. *on*. Cf. the phrases *leuest on*, believest in, l. 342; *leue on*, believe in, l. 795. The word *in* in l. 815 is exactly equivalent to the word *on* in l. 799.

825. *deyte*, divinity, divine presence. MS. B has *diet*. Supposing the author of the Crede to have written the Complaint of the Ploughman, we find his views expressed thus:—

"On our Lords body I doe not lie,
I say sooth through true rede,
His flesh and blood through his misterie
Is there, in the forme of brede:

How it is there it needeth not strive,
Whether it be subget or accident,
But as Christ was when he was on-live,
So is he there verament."—*Pol. Poems*, i. 341.

Such was the position of the Wycliffites. They denied the *extreme* form of the doctrine as declared by the friars, maintaining that whilst Christ was *bodily* present, the bread *never ceased to remain bread;* how this could be was a thing, they said, not to be explained. See Wycliffe's "Wicket."

847. The Complaint of the Ploughman ends in a very similar manner; the author even introduces the same word *avow* = guarantee, hold to.

"Witeth the pellican and not me,
For hereof I will not *avow*;
In high ne in low, ne in no degree,
But as a fable take it ye mowe.
To holy church I will me bow
Ech man *to amend him* Christ send space;
And for my writing me allow
He that is almighty for his grace."
Pol. Poems, i. 346.

GLOSSARIAL INDEX.

[*Abbreviations.* Prompt. Parv. = Promptorium Parvulorum (Camden Society); Cot. = Cotgrave's French Dictionary (1660); Glos. of Arch. = Glossary of Architecture; Piers Pl. = Piers Plowman (E. E. T. S., 1867); O. Fr. = Roquefort's Glossary of Old French; O.N. = Old Norse; &c.]

A-cast, cast off, cast away, 99.
Aferd, afraid, 130.
After þat, according as, 731, 732, 733.
A-gon, gone, spent, 624.
Aisliche, timorously, 341. Cf. Aȝleȝ=
Aȝles, fearless; *Gawayn*, l. 2335;
Aghlich = fearful, *do.* l. 136. A.S. *egeslice.*
Alabaustre, alabaster, 183.
Aldermen, elders, 691. See Rev. 4. 4.
Aloute, bow down, 750.
Als as, just as if (*contr. from* all-so-as), 378.
And, if, 393. And if (= an if), if, 17.
Angerlich, angrily, 268.
Anuell, a mass to be said annually; here, the money that pays for such a mass, 414.
Apert, open, plain; (or it may be an adv., openly, plainly), 541.
Asay, test; asay of, make trial of, 647.
Asaye, try (it), 247.
Assaie, power of testing, discrimination, 537.
Aunter, adventure. An aunter ȝif= it is an adventure if, it is a chance if; 789.
Auntrede, adventured; auntrede me, adventured myself, 341.
Auowen, avouch, warrant, 847. "*Advouer,* to advow, avouch, approve, allow of, warrant, authorize, &c." Cotgrave.

Awaytede, perceived, beheld, 172. O. Fr. *agaiter.*
Awyrien, curse, 662. A.S. *awyrian.*
Aȝen, again, 137.

Babelyng, babbling, 551.
Bacbyten, to backbite, 139.
Bale, woe, 696. A.S. *bealu.*
Bale, a pile, 667. "*Bǽl* (1) a funeral pile; (2) a burning." Bosworth.
Baly, belly, 763.
Bayteþ, bait, feed; in bayteþ, feed in, rummage in for food, 375. Chaucer.
Bedden, to provide with a bed, 772.
Beden, to offer, bestow on, 636.
Bedes, prayers, 389.
Bedys, beads, 323.
Been, bees, 727. A.S. *béo*, pl. *béon.*
Belded, builded, built, 548.
Belden, build, 706.
Beldinge, Beldyng, building, 501, 548.
Beleve, belief, 31.
Belliche, beautifully, 173.
Benen, beans, 762.
Benison, blessing, 654.
Beouten, without, 651. A.S. *bútan.*
Bernes, barns, 595.
Beslombred (*or* Beslomered), beslobbered, bedaubed, 427.
Betauȝte, commended; crist he me b., he commended me to Christ, 137. A.S. *betǽcan.*
Beþ, are, 254, 546; be ye (*imp.*), 442.
Beuer, beaver, 295.

Biclypped, embraced, covered, 227.
Biggeth, buy, 360. A.S. *bycgan*.
Bild, building, 157.
Biswynkeþ, labour for, get by labour, 722. A.S. *beswincan*.
Bledder, bladder, 222.
Bleynynge, blaining, 299.
Blisseþ, blesseth, 521.
Bode, an offer, proffer, bid, 716. See *Bode* in Jamieson. "Ye may yet war *bodes* or Beltan," ye may get worse offers ere Beltane-day (May 1); Ramsay's Scotch Prov. p. 83. Hence, to be at lone and bode = to deal with lendings and biddings, to lend and bid.
Bote, boot, remedy, 99, 335. A.S. *bót*.
Bragg, boastingly, 706.
Brenne, burn, 667.
Bretfull, quite full, 223. Swed. *brädd*, brim; *bräddful*, brimful.
Broche, a brooch or jewel, 323. "*Broche*, juelle." Prompt. Parv.
Brol, child, brat, 745, 748. "þe leeste barn (*another reading*, brol) of his blod," &c. Piers Pl. A. iii. 198.
Buldeþ, build, 118.
Burw3, a castle or large edifice; here, a convent, 118.
But, except, 554, 626.
Byforne, before, formerly, 612.
Byhirneþ, hide up in a corner, conceal, 642. See Hirnes.
Byhy3t, promised, 276.
Byiapeþ, bejape, deceive, 46.
Byleue, belief, the Creed, 16.
Bysynesse, busy toil, industry, 727.
Bythenk, reflect, 130.
Bytokneþ, betokens, 694, 696.

Can, (I) know, 8.
Canstou, knowest thou, 99.
Carefull, full of care, miserable, 441.
Cary, the name of a very coarse material, 422. Cf. "I-cloþed in a cauri-mauri." Piers Pl. A. v. 62.
Caste, planned, contrived, 486.
Casteþ, casts, i. e. contrives, plans; casteþ to-forn = plans beforehand, 485. See *caste* in Prompt. Parv.
Catell, goods, property, wealth, 116, 146, 283. O. Fr. *catels*. Low Lat. *catallum*.
Cautel, trickery, cunning, 303. O. Fr. *cautelle*; see *Romans of Partenay*, l. 5563.
Celle, cell, 739. "Applied sometimes to the small sleeping-rooms of the monastic establishments." Gloss. of Arch.
Chanons, canons, 674.
Chapaile, chapel, 119.
Chapolories, scapulars, 550. "Scaplorye (scapelary, scapelar) *Scapulare*." Prompt. Parv. And see Fairholt's costume in England, p. 595. Explained by Mr Wright to mean *chapeluries*, which I do not understand.
Chaptire, i. e. meeting of the chapter, 327.
Chaptire-hous, chapter-house, 199.
Chereliche, expensively, sumptuously, 582. Fr. *cher*.
Chesen, choose, 583; chesen hem to lustes, choose lusts, 684.
Cheuetyne, chieftain, lord, 582.
Childre, children, 756.
Chol, jowl; the part extending from ear to ear beneath the chin, 224. A.S. *ceolu*.
Chymene, chimney, 583. "This term was not originally restricted to the shaft, but included the fire-place." Gloss. of Arch.
Chymneyes, chimnies, 209.
Claweþ, stroke down, smooth down, 365. "*Flateur*, a flatterer, glozer, fawner, soother, foister, smoother; a *clawback*, sycophant, Pickthanke." Cotgrave.
Cloutede, patched, esp. used of strengthening a shoe with an iron plate, called in Norfolk a *cleat* or *clout*, 424.
Cloutes, clouts, patches, 244, 428; rags, tattered clothes, 438.
Cnaue, knave, lad, servant-man, 288.
Cnely, kneel (*infin.*), 124.
Cofren, to fasten up in a coffer or box, 68.
Cofres, coffers, boxes, 30.
Combren, 461,) to cumber, encumber; to gorge, 765.
Comeren, 765,)
Compased, went about, contrived, 635.

Conisantes, badges of distinction, 185.
Conne, know, learn, 101, 131, 234, 330, 395, 792; connen on, are acquainted with, 388. A.S. *cunnan*.
Cope, Copes; 126, 227, 292, 294, 724, 739.
Coruen, carved, 200.
Cotynge, cutting, 292.
Counfort, comfort, 99.
Couþe, could, 233.
Couþe, to make to know, to teach, tell, 17. A.S. *cýðan*.
Couþen, knew, 62. A.S. *cunnan*, pt. t. *ic cúðe*.
Crochettes, crockets, 174. "*Crockets*, projecting leaves, flowers, &c., used in Gothic architecture to decorate the angles of spires, canopies," &c. Gloss. of Arch. Du. *kroke*, a curl.
Crois, cross, 805.
Crombolle, crumbowl, prob. a large wooden bowl for broken scraps, &c., 437.
Cros, the cross, 1. See note.
Croukeþ, bend, bend down, 751.
Crucheþ, crouch, 751.
Curates, secular clergy who have *cure* of souls, 507.
Curious, dainty, 765.
Curry, rub down, stroke, 365. See *Curry* in Wedgwood's Etym. Dict.
Curtcis, courteous, gracious, 1, 140, &c. O. Fr. *courtois*.
Curteysliche, courteously, graciously, 637.
Cutted, cut short, 296, 434. Cf. Burns's "*cutty* sark" in *Tam o' Shanter*.

Defended, forbade, 576, 587, 669.
Deme, judge, 524.
Demen, to judge, 670, 814. A.S. *déman*.
Demest, judgest, 152.
Departen, to share goods; wiþ vs to departen, to share her goods among us, 416.
Deruelich, laboriously, industriously, 510. A.S. *deorfan*, *derfan*, to labour. See note.
Destruede, destroyed, i. e. put aside, 147.
Destruyeþ, destroy, 55.

Deyte, deity, 825.
Digne, dignified, haughty, disdainful (Chaucer), 355; disdainful, and hence repelling, repulsive, 375.
"Sche was as *deyne* as water in a dich,
As ful of hokir and of bissemare";
i. e. of frowardness and abusive speech. Chaucer, *Reeve's Tale*, 44.
Dissaucþ, deceiveth, 505.
Dortour, dormitory, 211.
Dotardes, dotards, 825.
Dranes, drones, 726. A.S. *drán*.
Dredles, doubtless, 524.
Drecchep, (*pl.*) vex, grieve, oppress, 464; (*sing.*) vexes, troubles, 504. A.S. *dreccan*.
Dued, endowed, endued with gifts, 776. Fr. *douer*.
Dygginge, digging, contriving, 504.

Egged, urged, 239. A.S. *eggian*, to incite.
Eiȝe, eye, 141, 142, 145, 288; *pl.* eiȝen, eyne, eyes, 84.
Eked, eked out, 244.
Elles, else, otherwise, 738.
Encombren, encumber, 483.
Ender, *in phr.* this ender daie = this day past, yesterday, lately, 239. Stratmann cites the German *ender* = Lat. *prius*, and O.N. *endr* = Lat. *olim*. Cf. Gower, C.A. i. 45.
Enfourme, inform, 272.
Entayled, sculptured, carved, 167, 200. O. Fr. *entailler*.
Er, ere, 374.
Erberes, gardens, 166. O. Fr. *herbier*. Lat. *herbarium*. [Distinct from harbour, A.S. *hereberga*.]
Erst, first, 242.
Euelles, evilless, without guilt, 242. [Prob. corrupt.]
Euesed, surrounded by clipped borders, 166. A.S. *efesian*, to clip like the eaves of a house.
Even-forþ, straightway, directly onwards, 163.
Eye, an egg, 225. A.S. *æg*.

Face, appearance, 670.
Falshede, Falshed, falsehood, falseness, 419, 682, 687.

GLOSSARIAL INDEX.   59

Falshedes, falsehoods, 616.
Faren, fare, go on, 775.
Fareþ, fare; fareþ wiþ, act with respect to, 728.
Fayntise, deceit, feigning, pretence, 251.
Faytoures, traitors, deceivers, 758. O. Fr. *faiturier*, a conjuror, from Lat. *factor*.
Fele, many, 547, 832; whou fele, how many, 522; so fele, so many men, 783; fele wise, many ways, 484.
Fen, muck, mire, 427, 429, 430. A.S. *fenn*.
Fend, fiend, 454, 460, 565, 577, 747; *pl.* fendes, fiends, 305.
Fer, far, 485.
Ferd, fared ; i. e. went, 203.
Fermery, 212, } an infirmary. Cf.
Fermori, 701, } *fermerere*, in Chaucer.
Ferrer, farther, 207.
Fet, fetched, 808.
Fcyne, feign, 273.
Feyþ, faith, 19, 95.
Fitchewes, fitchets, i. e. fitchets' fur, 295. A *fitchet* is a kind of polecat. Fr. *fissau*. O. Du. *vissche*. Called in Shropshire a *fitchuk*. See King Lear, A. iv. sc. 6, l. 124.
Fluricheþ, flourishes, varies capriciously, 484. [The idea is taken from making flourishes in illuminated drawings; cf. "Floryschyn' bokys. *Floro*." Prompt. Parv.]
Fond, attempt, endeavour, try, 95. A.S. *fandian*.
Fonded, tried, tested, 451.
Fonden, go, proceed, 338, 408. See *Lancelot of the Laik*.
Fonge, Fongen, to take, receive, get, catch, 146, 715; receive, take, get, 407, 786, 836. A.S. *fōn*. Ger. *fangen*. Mœso-Goth. *fahan*.
For, *used in the sense of* whether, if, 350; before, 613; against, 299.
Forbode, 415. Godys forbode = it is God's prohibition, God forbids. "Forbedynge, or forbode, or forefendynge. *Prohibicio, Inhibicio*." Prompt. Parv.
Forboden, forbidden, 147, 769. A.S.

forbodan, p.p. of vb. *forbeódan*.
For-deden, did to death, slew, murdered, 495. From the vb. *for-do*.
For-gabbed, scoffed at, 631. A.S. *gabban*, Swed. *begabba*.
Formfaderes, forefathers, 808. Cf. A.S. *forma*, former, early.
Forsoþe, for a truth, 148.
Forto, until, 311.
Forþan, for that (cause), on that account, 27. A.S. *forþan*.
For-werd, worn out, 429, 736. A.S. *forwered*.
Foundement, foundation, 250.
Foyns, martens, i. e. martens' fur. 295. "*Foviane*, the Foine, woodmartin, or beech-martin." Cotgr.
Fraitur, 212, } *See* Fraytour.
Fraitour, 701, }
Frayne, to question, 153.
Fraynede, questioned, asked, 28.
Fraynen, question, inquire of, 338. A.S. *fregnan*. Ger. *frayen*.
Fraynyng, a questioning, inquiry, 27.
Fraytour, a refectory or dining-room, 203, 284. Also spelt Fraitur, Fraitour, Freitour.
Freitour, 220. *See* Fraytour.
Freren, of friars, 311.
Freten, devour, 722, 729. A.S. *fretan*.
Furrynge, furs, 604.
Furste-froyt, first-fruits, 729.
Fyeþ on, cry shame on, 616.

Gabbynge, lying, deceit, 275. "Gabbynge, or lesynge. *Mendacium*." Prompt. Parv.
Gaped, stared, 156, 191. Ger. *gaffen*.
Garites, garrets, 214. See *Garyte* in Prompt. Parv.
Gaynage, profit, 197.
Generall, universal, catholic, 816.
Generallyche, universally, altogether, 575.
Gest, story, history, poem, 479. Lat. *gestum*. See note to Chaucer, l. 13775; ed. Tyrwhitt.
Gestes, stories, legends, 46.
Gilen, beguile, 599.
Gladding, pleasing, amusing, 515.
Glaueryuge, deceiving, deceitful, flattering, 51, 708. N. Prov. Eng.

glaiver, to talk foolishly; Welsh *ylafru*, to flatter.
Glees, songs, 93.
Gleym, bird-lime; hence, subtlety, craft, 479. Cf. l. 564. "Gleyme. *Limus, gluten.*" Prompt. Parv. Cf. Eng. *clammy*, prov. Eng. *clem.* See Wedgwood's Etym. Dict.
Gloppyng. *sb.* a swallowing greedily, a gulping down, 92. "Gloffare, or devowrare." Prompt. Parv.
Glose, *sb.* a gloss, a paraphrasing. a substitution of glosses for the text, 275, 515. See Prompt. Parv.
Glose, *vb.* mislead, deceive, 367.
Gloseþ, glosseth, explains away by glosses, 345, 383.
Glosinge, paraphrasing, 709.
Gut, a glutton. 67. A.S. *gluto.*
Godspell, gospel, 345; *pl.* Godspelles, Godspells, 257, 275, 709.
Goldbeten, adorned with beaten gold, 158.
Gome, a man, 585; *pl.* Gomes, men, 67, 282. A.S. *guma*, Lat. *homo.*
Good, goods, property, wealth, 22, 51, 54, 67, &c.
Gos, a goose; gos eye, a goose's egg, 225.
Gost, spirit, 521, 529; the Spirit, 590.
Graiþ, the plain truth, the truth, 34. See Grayþely = truly, *Allit. Poems,* C. 240; ed. Morris, E. E. T. S. From O.N. *greitha*, to make ready, explain.
Graith, *adv.* readily, 232. [It seems put for graith way = ready or direct road; Piers Pl. A. i. 181.]
Grayþed. prepared, 732. See Graiþ.
Grayþliche, readily, truly, 529. See Graith.
Grete, *adv.* greatly, 501.
Greyn, grain, 230.
Grysliche, terribly, horribly, very wickedly, 585. A.S. *yrislic.*

Halp, helped, 508.
Halt, holdeth, 345.
Halwen, hallow, 356.
Han, have, 569.
Harlotes, men of lewd life, ribalds, riotous men, 52 (where it is the gen. pl.), 766, 781. [*Harlot* is a term generally applied to men; cf. Chaucer, Prol. l. 647.]
Harlotri, riotous conduct, evil mode of life, 63.
Haylsede, saluted, 231. A.S. *healsian.*
He, she, 703. A.S. *héo.* See Ho.
He, they, 471. A.S. *hí, hie.*
Heer, hair, 423.
Heiȝe, *adv.* on high, 404, 551.
Hele, health, salvation, 264, 573.
Hem, *dat. pl.* to them, 58, 71, &c.; *acc. pl.* them, 79, 96, &c.
Hemselue, themselves, 42.
Hendliche, politely, *lit.* handily, 231. A.S. *gehende.*
Henten, get, lay hands on, catch hold of, seize, 413, 642. A.S. *hentan.*
Her, Here, their, 29, 31, 684, &c. A.S. *hira.*
Heraud, herald, 179.
Herberwe, to harbour, i. e. to lodge, 215.
Herdeman, a shepherd, pastor, 231.
Heremita, hermit, 308.
Hertliche, heartily, 325.
Hestes, commandments, 26, 345.
Heþen, hence, 408.
Heued, head, 317; (*pl.*?) heads (?), 773. A.S. *héafod*, pl. *héafdu.*
Heyȝ, high, 204.
Heynesse, highness, haughtiness, 265, 356, 542.
Hire, her, it, 782. Used with reference to *rewle;* cf. Lat. *regula*, a rule, *fem.*
Hirnes, corners, 182. A.S. *hirne.*
Hiȝede, hied, hastened, 155.
Ho, she, 411, 412, 415. A.S. *héo.*
Hobelen, go about clumsily, wander or "loaf" about, 106. [It does not imply lameness, but awkwardness; see Piers Pl. A. i. 113.]
Hod, hood, 423.
Hokschynes, (perhaps) gaiters, 426. Cf. *hoeshins, hushions*, gaiters (Jamieson). Perhaps = *hos-kins*, from *hose.* (Or *hok-synes* = hock-sinews.)
Holly, holy, 595, 836; holly tyme, holiday time, time after harvest, 595.
Hollich, Holliche, Hollyche, Holly, wholly, 26, 276, 678, 796, 815.

Homly, Homliche, in a homely way, plainly, 703; comfortably, 771.
Hondlen, handle, 108.
Honged, hung, 429.
Hongen, hang, bend over (*infin.*), 421.
Hongeþ, hang, 739.
Hordome, whoredom, 766.
Huny, honey, 726. A.S. *hunig*.
Hyen, 409, }
Hyȝe, 412, } hie, hasten.
Hyre, her, it; said of the soul, 668. [A.S. *sáwul* is *fem.*]
Hyȝe, high, 208, 210. *See* Heiȝe.

The words beginning with I- *are here collected; see also under* Y.
I-called, called, 574.
I-coruen, cut, carved, 161.
I-failed; is i-failed, hath failed, 98.
I-founded, founded, 47.
I-lyke, like, 546. A.S. *gelíc*.

Iapers, jesters, mockers, 43.
Iapes, mockeries, deceits, tricks, 47.
Ich, I, 155.
Ich a, Iche a, each, 109, 432, 702, 850.
Ichon, each one, 476.
Ijs, ice, 436. A.S. *ís*.
Iugulers, tricksters, 43. See note to Chaucer, l. 11453; ed. Tyrwhitt.

Kareyne, carrion, 644.
Knopped, full of knobs or bunches, 424. See *knobbe* and *knobbyd* in Prompt. Parv.; in the editor's note we find "A *knoppe* of a scho, *bulla*."
Knottes, knots, 161. "*Knot*, a boss, a round bunch of leaves, &c. The term is also used in reference to the foliage on the capitals of pillars." Gloss. of Arch.
Kundites, conduits, 195.
Kychens, kitchens, 210.
Kynde, *adj*. natural, 489; kynde ypocrites, hypocrites by nature.
Kynde, *sb*. nature, 834; of kynde, by nature, 43; natural occupation, 760.
Kynrede, kindred, 486.
Kyrtel, kirtle, 229. A.S. *cyrtel*.

Lacche, get, catch, acquire, 598. A.S. *læccan*.

Lakke, defame, 540; blame, find fault, 538. "Somwhat *lakken* hym wolde she." Rom. of the Rose, 284. Du. *laken*.
Latun, latoun or latten, a name given to a mixed metal much resembling brass, 196. See note to *Laton* in Prompt. Parv.
Launceþ, launch out with, fling abroad, 551. Fr. *lancer*, to fling.
Lauoures, lavers, 196. "A cistern or trough to wash in." Gloss. of Arch. [Often of a large size.]
Lawȝe, laugh, 94.
Lechures, lechers, 44.
Leed, lead, 193.
Lecl, leal, faithful, 390.
Leesinges, lies; leesinges lycþ, they lie their lies, 379. Cf. Lesynges.
Leeue, believe, 363, 372, 390.
Leeuen, live, 359.
Leeueþ, believeth, 15; believe, 639.
Lef, dear, 372. Cf. Leue.
Lefte, remained, 374.
Lel, leal, true, 344. Cf. Lecl.
Lellich, Lelliche, Lelly, Lellyche, leally, truly, faithfully, 235, 384, 639, 722.
Lemmans, mistresses, 83; lemmans holden = keep mistresses, 44. A.S. *léof*, dear, *man*, a person (male or female).
Lene, Lenen, lend, grant, give, 445, 741. A.S. *lǽnan*, to lend, give. See also Leue.
Lengeden, continued long, dwelt, 310.
Lenten, Lent, 11; *gen*. Lentenes, 568.
Lere me, teach me the way to, commend me to, 343.
Lered, learned, 18, 25.
Lerne, teach, 402.
Lesþ, loseth, 15.
Lesten, last, 855.
Lesynges, leasings, lies, 593.
Letten, let, hinder, 346.
Leue, dear, 390. Cf. Lef.
Leue, believe, 524. Cf. Leeue.
Leuede, believed, 235; *pl*. Leueden, believed, 25, 62. [*In* l. 25 *a better reading is* lecueþ; *cf*. l. 15.]
Leuest, liefest; leuest me were, would be most as I wish, 16.

Leuest, believest, 312.
Leueþ, believe, 039, 754.
Lewed, Lewede, unlearned, lay, common, 18, 25, 568, 832.
Leyen, lay (pt. t. of *to lie*), 187.
Leyest, Lext, liest, 541. [There is no difference of meaning between the two forms, and it was usual to *repeat* the words in this phrase : cf. " Til thow lixt and thou lixt lopen out at ones." Piers Pl. ed. Wright, p. 86.]
Leyne, to lend to, bestow money on (without expecting it back), 544. *See* Lene.
Libben, live, 700.
Libbeþ, live, 475, 610.
Liggeþ, lie, 83. A.S. *liggan.*
Liste; hem liste = it pleased them, 165. Cf. l. 71.
Loken, look out, find out, choose, 593.
Lollede, lolled about, wagged about, 224. " And lyk a leþerne pors *lullede* his chekes." Piers Pl. A. v. 110.
Lollede, called nim *loller*, spoke of him as *lolling*, 532. See the note.
Lone, a loan, a lending, 716. *See* Bode.
Lordynges, lords, 609.
Lore, teaching, 640.
Lorels, abandoned wretches, good-for-nothing fellows, 44, 721, 755. From A.S. *léosan*, pp. *loren*, to lose. Cf. Losels.
Loresmen, teachers, 290.
Losels, Losells, abandoned wretches, worthless fellows, 96, 597, 750. 827. A.S. *léosan*, to lose. Cf. Lorels.
Loþere, more loath, less willing. 544.
Louerd, Lord, 795.
Louren, look sourly, look displeased, 556. Du. *louren ;* cf. Sc. *glowre.*
Loutede, stooped, knelt, 333. A.S. *hlútan.*
Lowynge, humbling, 568. " Lowyn or mekyn. *Humilio.*" Prompt. Parv.
Lulling, *sb.* a lulling, a singing such as hushes one to sleep, 77. " Lullynge of yonge chylder. *Nenacio.*" Prompt. Parv.

Lust, pleasure, 700. A.S. *lust.*
Lust, Luste, it pleases, (*with dat.*) 71, 301. A.S. *lystan.*
Lybben, to live, 512. A.S. *lybban.*
Lybbeþ, live, 45, 110, 477.
Lyken, please, 77.
Lyknes, a likeness, i.e. a parable, 263.
Lymitour, a limitor, a friar who begs within a limited district, 597.
Lym-ȝerde, a limed twig, such as birds are caught with, 564. Cf. Gleym.
Lyuede, lived, 235 ; *pl.* Lyueden, 310.

Madde, art mad, 41 ; am mad, 280. [Observe its use as a neuter verb, without *to be.*]
Maistrely, like a master or doctor, 847.
Malisons, curses, 718.
Mansede, wicked, sinful, 718. A.S. *mán*, a crime.
Masedere, more in a maze, more confused, 826.
Maystri, mastery, dominion, 578.
Mede, reward, 533, 712, 715.
Mel, meal, 109.
Mendynauns, mendicants, beggars, 66.
Menc, mean ; *mene mongcorn*, corn of a common and mixed sort, 786. Cf. A.S. *mengan*, to mix.
Menelich, meanly, 108.
Mensk, grace, favour, (*lit.* humanity), 81. From A.S. *mennisc*, human.
Merciable, merciful, 629.
Merkes, marks, badges, tokens, 177.
Meseles, lepers, 623. O.Fr. *mesel ;* Lat. *miser, misellus.*
Mete, lit. moderate, middling ; hence, tight, scanty, insufficient, 428. Cf. the A.S. phrase " micle and mæte," great and small; Guthlac, l. 24 ; ed. Grein.
Misdou hem, commit trespass, transgress, 630.
Money-worþe, money's worth, 715.
Moneþ, month, 248.
Mong-corn, mixed corn, 786. See Mene.
Morþer, *sb.* murder, 635.
Morþeren, *vb.* to murder, 666.
Mot, Mote, 121, 520, 557, 591. It is difficult to give the *exact force ;* it more nearly answers to our modern

phrase *must needs* than to *may* or *must*; it is the A.S. *ic mót*, of which *ic móste*, I *must*, is the *past* tense.
Munte, *vb. refl.* mounted, went, 171.
Mychel, mickle, much, 55, 94, 673.
Myddel-erde, the middle-earth, i. e. the earth, the world, 535; *gen.* myddel-erde, of the world, in the world, 35. A S. *middan-geard*.
Myracles, miracle-plays, 107.
Myschef, mishap, accident; at myschef, by accident, 623.
Myster, kind, sort, 574. See Halliwell. *Lit.* a trade, occupation, O. Fr. *mestier*, Lat. *ministerium*.
Myteynes, mittens, 428.
Myȝtestou, Myȝt-tou, mightest thou, 123, 141. [Of these, the former follows the A.S. *indicative*, the latter the *subjunctive* mood.]

Ne, nor, 628; ne—ne, neither—nor, 80. A.S. *ne*.
Nemne, name, call, 472; nemne þe nouȝt, call thee a thing of naught, 540.
Noblich, nobly, 128.
Nolde (= ne wolde), would not, 190, 198.
Nones, in phr. for the nones, i. e. for the nonce, for the once, for the occasion, 183, 185. *Corrupted from* A.S. *for þan ánes*. [See Ormulum, ed. White, v. ii. p. 642.]
Nyl (= ne wyl), will not, 249.

O, one, one and the same, 440, 441. See Oo.
On, one, 789.
On, upon, in, 342, 795, 799, 822. A.S. *on*.
Ones, once, 491. A.S. *ánes*.
Oneþe, scarcely, 217.
Onliche, Onlie, singularly, specially, in a singular and special way, 534; in a way of their own, 610. Cf. A.S. *ǽnlíc*.
Oo, a, one; oo poynt, one bit, one jot, 198.
Opon, upon, 90, 103, &c.
Orcheȝardes, orchards, or rather, gardens, 166. A.S. *ort-geard*.

Oþer, either, 676; or, 62, 480, 712, 747, 757. A.S. *oððe*.

Palke, written for Pakke, pack, 399. (We often find *lk* written for *kk*.)
Paraunter, peradventure, 845. See l. 846.
Parten, to impart, give away, 301.
Pasen, Passen, to surpass, 666; to go beyond, surpass, 710, 711; go too far, 846.
Passeþ, surpasseth, 834; passeþ pursutes, surpass all persecutions (by others), 664.
Patred, repeated constantly, said over and over again, 6. See note.
Paynt, painted, 121.
Pekokes, peacocks, 764.
Penounes, pennons, small banners, 562. "Penonc, lytylle banere." Prompt. Parv.
Pertriches, partridges, 764.
Peynt, painted, 192; peynt til, painted tiles, 194. This is better than poynt til = pointed tiles, square tiles. See note.
Pilche, a fur garment, or garment of skin with the hair on, 243. Lat. *pellis, pellicea*.
Pild, bald, 839. See *Pyllyd* in Prompt. Parv.; and cf. "*Peel'd* priest" in Shakesp. I. Henry VI. Ac. I. sc. 3, l. 30.
Plouers, plovers, 764.
Plyȝt, plighted, 240.
Pomels, pommels, 562. "*Pomel*, a knob, knot, or boss; the term is used in reference to a finial, or ornament on the top to a conical or a dome-shaped roof of a turret," &c. Gloss. of Arch.
Portred, portrayed. adorned, 192.
Possessioners, possessioners, 681. See note.
Pouere, poor, 521, 567.
Pouerte, poverty, 113.
Powghe, pouch, or box, 618. *See* Terre.
Poynt, Poynte, piece, part, 6; piece, bit, 194; oo poynt = one bit, a single jot, 198.
Poyntes, points, 562. [In an heraldic sense.]
Prese, press, press forward, 749.

Prest, ready, 288. O. Fr. *prest*, Fr. *prêt*.
Pris, chief, excellent; her pris lijf, i. e. the best part of their life, 621.
Prijs, chief, 256. [It seems here to be an *adjective*, as in l. 621.]
Propre, own, 569.
Proue, *vb.* test, 247. Proue and asaye = test and try it.
Pryuitie, secret working, 834.
Pulched, polished, 121, 160. "Pulchon. *Polio;*" Prompt. Parv.
Pulpit, 661.
Puple, people, 66, 74, 87, 713, &c.
Pure litel, very little, 170; pure myte, a mere mite, 267.
Purliche, purely, 270; hence, completely, altogether, 319, 331, 713.
Purse, bag, 301.
Pursut, persecution; pursut of = persecution by, 655.
Pursueþ, persecute, 664.
Pylion, a sort of cap used by priests, esp. by cardinals, 830. Ital. and Span. *pileo*, Lat. *pileus*.

Quenes, women, queans, 84. A.S. *cwén*.
Queynt, Queynte, cunning, sly, 303, 452; cunningly contrived, curious, 552.
Queyntise, Queyntyse, sleight, cunning, craft, 388, 507. "Queyntyse, or sleythe. *Astucia.*" Prompt. Parv.
Queynteli, curiously, 161.
Quyk, in phr. quyk myre = moving mire, quagmire, 226. [*Lit.* a live mire.]
Qnyten, quit, requite with, 351.

Rageman, a catalogue, a list, 180. See *Rugman Roll* in Jamieson.
Raken, wander, rove about, 72. O.N. *reika*, to ramble.
Randes, strips, slices, 763. "To cut me into *rands* and sirloins." Beaumont & Fletcher. *Wildgoose Chase*, Ac. V. sc. 2. "*Giste de bœuf*, a *rand* of beef, a long and fleshy peece, cut out from between the flanke and buttock." Cotgr.
Rauȝt, reached, obtained, 733.
Redeliche, 811, } readily, speedily.
Rediliche, 809, }

Respondes, responds, 377.
Reufull, miserable, in pitiful condition, 432.
Reuthe, pity, 738.
Rewle, rule (of an order), 377, 536.
Rewme, realm, 774.
Ribaut, ribald, worthless fellow, 376.
Roþeren, rothers, heifers, 431. A.S. *hryðer*.
Rychesse (*sing.*), riches, 733.
Ryȝt-lokede, righteous, just, 372. Apparently corrupted from A.S. *rihtlic*; cf. note to l. 684.

Say, saw, 158.
Schaf, chaff, 663.
Schenden, ruin, disgrace, blame, 481, 677. A.S. *scendan*.
Schendeþ, ruin, 488.
Schendyng, *sb.* reproof, disgrace, disgraceful end, 94.
Schent, blamed, reproved, 9.
Scheten, shut, shut up, enclose, 773.
Schon, shoon, shoes, 209, 424, 735, 733.
Se, a seat, 558.
Segge, say, 703.
Selȝ, saw, 208, 421.
Selles, cells, 60. *See* Cell.
Selure, a decorated ceiling, 201. Lat. *cælatura*. See note to "Ceelyn with syllure. *Celo*" in Prompt. Parv.
Sely, poor, simple, 442, 444, 668, 672, 675. A.S. *sǽlig*, happy, blessed.
Semliche, seemly, comely, 201.
Sepultures, burials, buryings, 469.
Seþ, see, 652.
Sexe, six, 739.
Seweden, followed, pursued, 531.
Sey, saw, 146. [Prob. an error for *se* = see.]
Seyn = say, 25, 56, 85.
Sikerli, for a certainty, with certainty, 64. "Sykyr, (or serteyne)." Prompt. Parv.
Siþe, Siþen, Siþþe, since, 158, 353; seeing that, 259. A.S. *siðða*.
Siȝede, sighed, 442.
Slauþe, sloth, 91. Another reading is *slaughte*, destruction.
Slen, to slay, 668.
Slomerers, slumberers, 91.

GLOSSARIAL INDEX.

Soget, subject, 650.
Sorweþ, sorroweth, 688.
Soþ, true, 841, 842.
Soþe, sooth, truth, 364, 388, 658, 794.
Soþfast, true, very, 822.
Soutere, cobbler, 744, 752. Lat. *sutor.*
Sowle hele, health of the soul, 680.
Spedfullest, readiest, 264.
Spicerie, spicery, spices, 301.
Sprad, spread, scattered loosely, 301.
Stappyng, stepping, 649.
Stei3, ascended, 810. A.S. *stígan,* pt. t. *ic stáh.*
Stere, stir, 829.
Sterue, Steruen, die, 69, 740. A.S. *steorfan.*
Stodyen, study, 588.
Ston, rock, 806, 810.
Strakeþ, roam, wander wide, (*lit.* stretch), 82.
Stre, straw, 773.
Stues, stews, 631.
Stumblen, stumble about, 591.
Sturen, stir, 588.
Stynkande, stinking, 649.
Sty3tle, to set in order, direct, 315. A.S. *stihtan.*
Suen, follow, 60, 105. O.Fr. *suir.*
Sueres, followers, 148.
Sueþ, follow, 454.
Suffraunce, patience, 652. "*Bele vertue est* suffraunce." Piers Plowm. ed. Whitaker; p. 225.
Suffrant, patient, 646.
Suffreþ, endure, 650.
Sustren, sisters, 85, 329.
Suweþ, follow, 577. *See* Sueþ.
Swiche, such, 519.
Swyþe, very, 622.
Sy3ge, say, 390.
Syker, safe, secure, 306, 350; *adv.* surely, certainly, 237, 704; *superl.* Sykerest, surest, securest, best, 277.
Synagoges, synagogues, 558.
Syþen, since, 241; afterwards, 668, 806.

Tabernacles, cells for reconnoitring, 168.
Tatered, jagged, 753.

Tempren, temper, subdue, mortify, 743.
Terre, in phr. terre pow3e, 618. Mr Wright says, "a torn sack or poke (?)" The old glossary to the edition of 1553 suggests "tar box;" and I think it is right; only, strictly speaking, a *pow3he* is a *pouch. Terre* is the usual old spelling of *tar;* see Prompt. Parv.; and in Halliwell, s. v. Tarbox, we find—"a box used by shepherds for carrying tar, used for anointing sores in sheep, marking them, &c. *Tarre boyste* = tar box, occurs in Chester Plays, i. 125."
Þei3, though, 69.
Þere as, there where, 471.
Þis, þies, these, 290, 392.
Þo, those, 96, 619, 853. A.S. *þá.*
Þolede, suffered, 90, 823. A.S. *polian.*
Tildeth, set up, 494. *See* Tyld.
To-forn, before, beforehand, 485.
Tonne, tun, 221.
Too, toe, 649.
Toten, to see clearly, perceive, 142; to look out, spy round, 168; *pt. t.* Totede, looked, 339; *pl.* Toteden, in phr. toteden out = peeped out, 425. "Totebylle, *Specula.*" Prompt. Parv. *Totyng-place* is a watchtower; Wycliffe's Bible; Isaiah xxi. 5.
Touche, the sense of touch, 537.
Trechurly, treacherously, 475.
Treddede, trod, walked over, 425.
Trofle, trifle, 352. [*Trefle* in the old printed text; but MS. A has the spelling *trofle.* O.Fr. *trufle,* a trifle; *trufler,* to mock, cheat.]
Troiflardes, triflers, cheats, 742. Cf. l. 475.
Trosten, *vb.* trust, 237; on to trosten, to trust in, 350.
Trussen, pack up, 618.
Tweie, Twey, Tweyne, two, 428, 439.
Twyes, twice, 178.
Twynnen, to count as twins, to consider alike, 496.
Tyld, set up like a tent, set up, raised, 181. A.S. *teldian,* to spread a tilt or tent.

Tylyen, to till, 743. A.S. *tilian*.
Tymbren, build, 723. A.S. *timbrian*.
Tymen, bring, induce, compel, 742. Compare *temen*, in Chaucer, House of Fame, 1744.
Tyn, tin, 195.
Tynt, lost, 537. O.N. *týna*.

Vndernepen, underneath, 695.
Vnnepe, scarcely, with difficulty, 45. A.S. *un-éaðe. See* Onepe.
Vnteyned, unfastened, not grounded, 516. A.S. *týnan;* see note. [It should rather have been spelt Vntyned.]
Vsen, use, 63.
Vsep, use, 690, 693, 697.

Wagged, wagged about, 226.
Waite, pay heed, look, 361. O.Fr. *gaiter. See* Awaytede.
War, wary; ben war, beware, 844.
Warlawes, deceivers, 783. Sc. *warlo*, A.S. *wǣrloga*, a word-breaker, liar. Prob. *distinct* from Sc. *warluwe*, a warlock; see *warlo, warluwe* in Jamieson.
Waryep, curseth, 615. A.S. *wærgian*.
Waseled, bemired himself, 430. From O.E. *waise, wose*, A.S. *wós*, ooze, mud.
Waspe, wasp, 648.
Wayuen, to waive, give up, cast aside, 530, 685. O.Fr. *guesver*, to a-bandon; cf. *guerpir*, Ger. *werfen*. See *Guesver* in Cotgrave and Roquefort.
Wele, weal, wealth, 20, 403, 784.
Wende, weened, expected, 32, 452.
Werche, Werchen, *vb.* work, 260, 285, 527, 783.
Werdliche, 371, worldly. [*Werld* is often spelt *werd* in O. English.]
Werwolues, werwolves, 459.
Wexen, wax, become, 525.
Whiʒt, 32, }
Whit, 430, } a wight.
Whou, Whow, Whouʒ, how, 42, 141, 192, 234, 365.
Whyʒtes, wights, 812.
Wichep, wisheth, 615.
Wijt, wit, 833, 854.
Wijʒt, a wight, man, 233; *see* Wiʒt.

Wil, while, 416.
Wilne, will (*pl.* of wil), 216.
Wilnest, desirest, 676.
Wilnep, *sing.* desireth, 20; *pl.* desire, covet, 361, 371, 497, 499. A.S. *wilnian*.
Wissen, to make to know, to teach, 100, 233. A.S. *wissian*.
Wist, known, 452.
Wip, with; to coueren wip our bones = to cover our bones with, 116; toilen wip = bestow toil on, 742.
Wiʒt, a wight, man, 17.
Wiʒt, a whit; a litil wiʒt = a little whit, ever so little, 538.
Wlon, hems, hemmed borders(?), 736. A.S. *wlo*, a fringe, hem, border; whence perhaps *wlon* is formed as a plural, like *schon* and *been*. Or else we may adopt the reading *wolne* (MS. B) = wool, nap; only *wolne* would more properly be an *adj.* = *woollen*.
Wolward, 788. "*Wolwarde*, without any lynnen next ones body, *sans chemyse*." Palsgrave. To go *woolward* was a common way of doing penance, viz. with the *wool towards* one's skin.
Wombe, belly, 762.
Wone, dwelling-place, 164.
Wonynge, dwelling, 768.
Woon, a dwelling-place; hence, a building, 172.
Wordlyche, worldly, 784. *See* Werdliche.
Wortes, worts, 787; wortes fleches wroughte, vegetables cooked without meat.
Worpe, Worpen, become, be, be made, 748, 826, 828; to become, to be, 9, 580, 776; *pp.* become, 431 (see note); to happen, in phr. wo mote ʒou worpen, may wo happen to you, evil be to you, 493. A.S. *weorðan*.
Worp to, become, 746. *See* Worpe.
Worpely, worthy, estimable, 233. A.S. *wurðlic*.
Wouʒ, how, 356. *See* Whou.
Wynwe-schete, a sheet used in winnowing corn, 435.
Wyten, to know, 32. A.S. *witan*.

The following are the past participles, &c., beginning with Y-; see also under I.

Y-benched, furnished with benches or seats, 205.
Y-beld, built, 172. *See* Y-buld.
Y-blessed, blessed, 520.
Y-botend, buttoned, 296.
Y-bouʒt, bought, 569.
Y-buld, built, 157. *See* Y-beld.
Y-clense (*inf.*), to cleanse, 760.
Y-cloþed, clothed, 608.
Y-corven, carved, 173.
Y-couenaunt, covenanted, 38.
Y-crouned, crowned, 805.
Y-diʒte, Y-dyʒt, fitted up, provided, 211; prepared, made, 228. A.S. *dihtan*, to arrange.
Y-founde, founded, 242.
Y-founden, found, 631.
Y-gadered, gathered, 189.
Y-greiþed, prepared, fitted, 196; made ready, 626. *See* Graiþ.
Y-hamled, cut off short, docked, 300. "Algate a foot is *hameled* of thi sorwe." Chaucer; Troil. & Cress. ii. 138. A.S. *hamelian*.
Y-hid, hid, 643.
Y-hyled, covered, 193. A.S. *helan*.
Y-knowen, Y-cnowen, known, 252, 800; know (*inf.*), 647.
Y-leyd, laid, 263.
Y-lich, alike (*adj.*), 730.
Y-maked, made, 93.
Y-medled, placed in the middle, placed alternately (with other things, i.e. with the shields), 177.
Y-noumbred, numbered, 178.
Y-paynted, painted, 506.
Y-paued, paved, 194.
Y-peynt, Y-peynted, painted, 160, 202.
Y-rade, read, 129.
Y-rosted, roasted, 764.
Y-sacred, consecrated, sanctified, 186.
Y-set, set, 201, 315, 761.
Y-sewed, sewn, 229.
Y-stongen, pierced, pricked through (*lit.* stung), 553.
Y-suled, soiled, sullied, 752. A.S. *sylian*. Dan. *söle*.
Y-tiʒt, firmly fastened, fixed, set, 168. *Lit.* tied, from A.S. *tigan*. Spenser uses *tight* for *tied*.
Y-toted, inspected, 219. *See* Toten.
Y-vsed, used, 510.
Y-wis, certainly, 555. Cf. Ger. *gewiss*.
Y-worþen, become, 665; *see* Worþen.
Y-wrouʒt, wrought, 162.

Ymped, grafted, 305. "Impyd or graffed. *Insertus*" Prompt. Parv.
Yuele, *adv.* evilly, 660; ill, 58.

ʒemede, looked carefully; ʒemede opon = closely regarded, 159. A.S. ʒȳman, to pay heed to.
ʒerne, diligently, 159.
ʒif, if, 62, &c.
ʒyuen, to give, 54.
ʒyueþ, give, 114.

INDEX OF NAMES.

Austen, St Augustine, 579, 777.
Austyn, an Augustine friar, 239; Austyns, 268.
Austynes, St Augustine's, 466, 509.
Aue-marie, 7.

Brut, Wat; Walter Brute, 657.

Carm, Carmelite, 38, 39; *see* Karmes.
Carmeli, Mt Carmel, 57.
Caym, Cain, 486; *see* Kaymes.
Charthous, Carthusians, 674.
Crede, 8, 36, 38, 101, 131, 234, 272, 343, 448, 792.
Credo ; the first word of the Creed, 795.
Crist, 1, 37, 57, 62, &c.
Cristen, Christian, 41, 382, 792; Christians, 470, 669.
Christendam, 30, 278, 481.

Domynike, St Dominick, 353, 464, 510, 579, 776.

Elves, Elias', Elijah's, 383.

Farysens, Pharisees, 487, 547
Four orders, 29, 153, 284, 451.
Fraunces, seynt, 126, 291, 293, 298, 465, 511, 579, 775.

Golias, 479.

Helye, Elijah, 777.
Herdforthe, Hertford, 362.
Holy Gost, 802, 815, 836.
Hyldegare, St Hildegarde, 703.

Jesu, 14, 575, 799.

Jewes, 14.

Karmes, Carmelites, 338, 340, 382.
Kaymes, Cain's, 559.

Lady; Our Lady, 77, 79, 384.
Lenten, Lent, 11, 568.
Lucifer, 374, 578.

Marie, 270, 803.
Maries-men, 48.
Menoure, Minorite, 33, 40, 276.
Menures, Minorites, 103, 381.
Minoures, Minorites, 281.

Parlement-hous, 202.
Paternoster, 6, 336.
Paul (the hermit), 308.
Peres (the plowman), 473, 482, 679, 791.
Petur, St Peter, 710.
Popes, 256, 467.
Powel, Paul, 80, 87.
Prechours, friars Preachers, Dominicans, 154, 348, 354, 373, 381, 386, 506.
Pye, freres of the, 65.

Robertes-men, Roberds-men or vagabonds, 72.
Rome, 46, 256, 467.

Satan, 480; Satanas, 717.

Trynitee, 127.

Wedenesday, 13.
Wycliff, 528.

God spede the Plough.

(Lansdowne MS. 762; fol. 5 a.)

A PROCESSE OR AN EXORTATION TO TENDRE THE
CHARGIS OF THE TRUE HUSBONDYS.

As I me walked ou*er* feldis wide [1]		As I went over the fields in ploughing time, I saw husbandmen at work, and said "God speed the plough!"
When men began to Ere and to Sowe,		
I behelde husbondys howe faste they hide,		
With their bestis and plowes all on A rowe;	4	
I stode and behelde the bestis well drawe		
To ere the londe that was so tough;		
Than to an husbond I sed this sawe,		
"I pray to God, spede wele the plough."	8	
The husbondys helde vp harte and hande,		One of them answered—"It is needful to say so; we have hard work of it."
And said, "that is nedefull for to praye;		
For all the yere we labour with the [lande],		
With many a comberous clot of [claye],[2]	12	
To mayntayn this worlde yf that we maye,		[Fol. 5 b.]
By downe and by dale and many a slough;		
Therfore it is nedefull for to saye,		
'I praye to God, spede wele the plough.'	16	

[1] This line is omitted in its right place; but is written perpendicularly on the inner margin of the leaf, with a guide-line to show its position.
[2] The corner of the leaf is torn away.

The parson gets the tithe-sheaf.	And so shulde of right the parson praye,	
	That hath the tithe shefe of the londe;	
We have to pay our servants, and the clerk and sexton want something.	For our sarvauntys we Moste nedis paye,	
	Or ellys ful still the plough maye stonde.	20
	Than cometh the clerk anon at hande,	
	To haue A shef of corne there it groweth;	
	And the sexten somwhate in his hande;	
	'I praye to God, spede wele the plough.'	24
The king's purveyors want wheat and meat,	The kyngis puruiours also they come,	
	To haue whete and otys at the kyngis nede;	
	And over that befe and Mutton,	
	And butter and pulleyn, so god me spede!	28
and we must give it, and be paid with a beating.	And to the kyngis courte we moste it lede,	
	And our payment shalbe a styk of A bough;	
	And yet we moste speke faire for drede—	
	'I praye to God, spede wele the plough.'	32
We have to pay the fifteenth, and our lord's rent;	To paye the Fiftene ayenst our ease,[1]	
	Beside the lordys rente of our londe;	
	Thus be we shepe shorne, we may not chese,	
	And yet it is full lytell vnderstonde.	36
also bailiffs and beadles.	Than bayllys and bedell*is* woll putto their hande	
	In enquestis to doo vs sorowe Inough,	
	But yf we quite right wele the londe—	
	['I][2] praye to God, spede wele the plough.'	40
Prisoners come and beg of us,	[Than come]th prisoners and sheweth their nede,	
	[What gret] sorowe in prison theye drye;	
	['To buye the kyngi]s pardon we most take hede'—	
[Fol. 6 a.]	For man and beste they woll take money.	44
and then come the clerks of St John.	Than cometh the clerke3 of saint Iohn Frary,	
	And rede in their bokis mennyis namyis inough,	
	And all they live by husbondrye—	
	'I praye to God, spede wele the plough.'	48

[1] MS. "eases."   [2] The corner of the leaf is torn away.

Then comme the graye Freres and make theire mone,
And call for money our soulis to save;
Then comme the white Freres and begyñ to grone,
Whete or barley they woll fayne haue; 52
Then commeth the freres Augustynes & begynneth to crave
Corne or chese, for they haue not Inough;
Then commeth the blak freres which wolde fayne haue—
'I praye to God, spede wele t[h]e plough.' 56

[margin: Then come Minorites, Carmelites, Augustines, and Dominicans.]

And yet, amongest other, we may not forgete
The poore obseruauntes that been so holy;
They muste amongis vs haue corne or mete,
They teche vs alwaye to fle from foly, 60
And liue in vertue full devowtely,
Preching dayly Sermondys inough
With good Examples full graciously—
'I praye to God, spede wele the plough.' 64

[margin: Then come the poor Observants to be paid for preaching.]

Than cometh the Sompner to haue som rente,
And ellis he woll teche vs A newe lore,
Saying, we haue lefte behynde vnproved som testament,
And so he woll make vs lese moche more. 68
Then commeth the grenewex which greveth vs sore,
With ronnyng in reragis it doth vs sorowe Inough,
And After, we knowe nother why ne where-fore—
'I praye to God, spede wele the plough.' 72

[margin: Then come the summoner, and the greenwax, which grieves us sore.]

Then commeth prestis that goth to rome
For to haue silver to singe at *Scala celi;*
Than commeth clerkys of Oxford and make their mone,
To her scole hire they most haue money. 76
Then commeth the tipped-staves for the Marshalse,
And saye they haue prisoners mo than Inough;
Then commeth the mynstrellis to make vs gle—
'I praye to God, spede wele the plough.' 80

[margin: Then come priests, and clerks of Oxford; [Fol. 6 b.] and tipstaves and minstrels.]

We have too to pay the lawyer for pleading;	At london Also yf we woll plete,
	We shal not be spared, good chepe nor dere ;
	Our man of lawe may not be forgete,
	But he moste haue money every quarte[re ;] 84
and to give to chartered beggars and weeping women."	And somme comme begging with the kyngis charter,
	And saye, bisshoppis haue graunted ther-to pardon
	Inough ;
	And wymen commeth weping on the same Maner—
	'I praye to God, spede wele the plough.' " 88
I thanked him, and prayed God to speed the plough, and all ploughmen.	And than I thanked this good husbond,
	And prayed God the plough to spede,
	And All tho that laboreth with the londe,
	And them that helpeth them with worde or dede. 92
	God¹ give them grace such life to lede,
	That in their concience maye be mery Inough,
	And heven blisse to be their mede,
	And ever I praye, "God¹ spede the plough." 96

¹⁻¹ MS. Gog.

NOTES.

The MS. (Lansdowne, 762) from which this poem is taken is a sort of album or collection of scraps, not all in the same handwriting. There is little doubt but that this copy of "God speed the Plough," belongs to the reign of Henry the Eighth, for in the same hand there is a table of Kings of England, with verses about them, which ends with saying that Henry the Seventh was buried at Westminster. At the same time, Mr Hamilton thinks the handwriting to be not very late, but to belong to the *early* part of Henry the Eighth's reign. The poem itself does not seem to be much earlier; and the complaints of the exactions made by the King's purveyors, bailiffs, beadles, the summoner and the "grenewex," seem particularly suitable to the reign of Henry the Seventh. As a conjectural date, A.D. 1500 may not be very far from the truth. Another poem, written much in the style of "Speed the Plough," has for its burden the line,

"London, thowe arte the flowre of cities all;" *(fol.* 8).

1. Even without the "guide-line," we can tell by the structure of the stanza that the line written in the margin is really l. 1. The 2nd, 4th, 5th, and 7th lines of each stanza rime together throughout.

22. *Groweth.* This seems a strange rime to *plough.* Perhaps it should be *growe* = grew.

28. Wright, in his Provincial Dictionary, quotes the following:—

"A false theefe

That came, like a false foxe, my *pullain* to kill and mischeefe."

Gammer Gurton, Old Pl. ii. 63.

43. The words within square brackets are conjectural, and were suggested by the fact recorded in Piers Plowman, that getting pardon for a bribe even from a King is not altogether a thing unknown; see Piers Pl. Text A. Pass. III. ll. 16—20, and IV. ll. 120--125 (ed. Skeat, 1867).

45. *Frary,* friary, fraternity; there was one such in Clerkenwell.

49. See note to the "Crede," l. 29. On fol. 9 *b* of this very Lansdowne MS. we find the following. "Fratres London. Whitefreres in fletestrete, Carmelitarum. Blak freres within ludgate, predicatorum *vel* Jacob: Greye freres within newgate, Minor*um.* Augusteyn freres by saint Antonyes, Augustinenci*um.* Crowched freres, Fratres sancte Crucis."

67. This line is too long. The word "*behynde*" is superfluous.

74. *Scala celi.* Compare—

"In þat place a chapelle ys,
Scala cely called hit ys,
'Laddere of henen' men clepeþ hit."
The Stacyons of Rome, in *Political, Religious, and Love Poems,*
p. 118 (E. E. T. S.)

On which Mr Rossetti has the note, "The chapel *Scala cœli* stands near the foregoing church of St Anastatius. It was built over the cemetery of St Zeno, and has undergone restorations from 1582 onwards. It derives its name from a vision of St Bernard's, who, while celebrating a funeral mass, saw the souls for whom he was praying going up to heaven by a ladder."

We should compare with this poem the feeling expressed in the Spanish proverb—"*Lo que no lleva Christo, lleva el fisco*"; that which Christ (i.e. the clergy) takes not, the exchequer carries away. Lines 75, 76 remind us of Chaucer's clerk of Oxenford, who

"busily gan for the soules pray
Of hem that gaf him wherewith to scolay."

85. These chartered beggars remind us of Edie Ochiltree, the King's Bedesman, with his blue gown and pewter badge, in Sir Walter Scott's novel of the Antiquary; see vol. I. ch. iv.

It should be noted that the word *plough* is made to rime with *tough, slough, groweth* (*growe?*), *bough,* and *inough* (8 times). The probable pronunciation seems to be the same as now-a-days, *slough* and *bough* being still admissible rimes. In the Trinity MS. of "Piers Plowman" (classmark R. 3. 14) there is a picture of two "husbondys" with a plough and two "bestis," with a motto written above, which runs—"God spede þe plouȝ & send us korne I-now"—where *I-now* represents the old pronunciation of *inough.* In the MS. of the same poem in Corpus Christi College, Cambridge, the same motto occurs, but without the picture.

GLOSSARIAL INDEX AND INDEX OF NAMES

TO

"GOD SPEDE THE PLOUGH."

Bayllys, bailiffs, 37.
Bedellis, beadles, 37.
Chepe, *in phr.* good chepe = at a good market, at a low price, 82.
Chese, choose, 35.
Drye, suffer, endure, 42. Sc. *dree*. A.S. *dréogan*.
Enquestis, inquiries, searches, 38.
Ere, to plough, 2, 6. A.S. *erian*. Lat. *arare*. *See* Isaiah xxx. 24; 1 Sam. viii. 12.
Fiftene, fifteenth, a tax amounting to a fifteenth of one's property, 33.
Frary, fraternity, 35. "*Frary clerk*, a member of a clerical brotherhood." Wright's Prov. Dict.
Freres, graye (Franciscans), 49; white (Carmelites), 51; Augustynes, 53; blak (Dominicans), 55.
Grenewex, 69. Greenwax was used for estreats delivered to the sheriffs out of the king's exchequer. These estreats were under the seal of that court, made in *greenwax*. *See* Blount's Law Dictionary.
Hide, hied, hastened, 3.

Husbond, husbandman, 7, 89; *pl.* husbondys, 3, 9.
Iohn, saint, 45.
Lese, lose, 68.
London, 81.
Marshalse, 77.
Obseruauntis, friars observauts, 58. " Observants, a branch of the Franciscan order, otherwise called *Recollects*." Imperial Dict.
Oxford, 75.
Plete, plead, 81.
Pulleyn, poultry, 28. Cf. *Pullayle* in Chaucer.
Quite, quit; i. e. pay rent for in full so as to be *quit*, 39.
Reragis, arrears, 70.
Rome, 73.
Scala celi, the name of a chapel in Rome, 74.
Sermondys, sermons, 62.
Sexten, sexton, 23.
Sompner, a summoner, 65.
There, where, 22.
Tipped-staves, tipstaves, constables, 77. So called from their bearing a staff tipped with metal.
Vnderstonde, understood, 36.

www.ingramcontent.com/pod-product-compliance
Lightning Source LLC
Chambersburg PA
CBHW020157170426
43199CB00010B/1078